The Whale

C000141812

The Whaler of Scotland Yard

Jock Murray

BIRLINN

First published in 2011 by
Birlinn Limited
West Newington House
10 Newington Road
Edinburgh
EH9 1QS

www.birlinn.co.uk

Copyright © Jock Murray, 2011

The moral right of Jock Murray to be identified as the author of this work has been asserted by him in accordance with the Copyright, Designs and Patents Act 1988

All rights reserved. No part of this publication may be reproduced, stored or transmitted in any form without the express written permission of the publisher

ISBN-13: 978 1 78027 017 3
eBook ISBN: 978-0-85790-087-6

British Library Cataloguing-in-Publication Data
A catalogue record for this book is available from the British Library

Set in Goudy Old Style at Birlinn

Printed and bound in Great Britain by
Clay-s Ltd, St Ives PLC

Contents

Illustrations

1

Lewis

I was born on the Isle of Lewis on Boxing Day 1940, twenty-two years after the end of the First World War. The Second World War was still in its infancy. I am told the Isle of Lewis lost more men per population in both wars than any other place in Britain, but I don't know whether this is true or not. My uncle Alasdair was drowned at the age of 19 when his ship, HMT *Neptunian*, was lost on the last day of World War One.

On New Year's Eve 1918, some 600 soldiers, sailors and airmen gathered in Kyle of Lochalsh, the mainland terminal for the ferry to Stornoway. They were returning from the trenches and the atrocities of the First World War. In a few hours they would be with their loved ones, and some of them had not been home since the beginning of hostilities. The local mail ferry to Stornoway, the *Sheila*, did not have the capacity to take so many passengers. The Admiralty or the War Office who they had served for the previous four years had made no arrangement for them to get across the Minch on their final journey home. HMY *Iolaire*, with a crew of 23, was directed to Kyle and the remaining 260, all naval ratings, boarded her.

Once on board the *Iolaire* they met friends and relations whom they had not seen since they left home at the beginning of the war. There must have been some rejoicing at having survived. Two hours after leaving Stornoway the New Year was celebrated on board and all were in good spirits. When Arnish lighthouse at the entrance to Stornoway harbour came in sight it was time to get ready for disembarking in Stornoway, where relatives and loved ones were gathering to welcome them home. However, this was not to be. All of a sudden, for some reason which was never established, the *Iolaire*, well off course, went aground on rocks in the entrance to the harbour known as the 'Beast of Holm'. The ship listed heavily to starboard in the dark and stormy night and she was pounded by waves. Some men jumped into the sea, but all who did were drowned.

Rockets that were fired showed they were only yards away from the shore, but the sea was so rough that anyone who tried to swim was crashed against the rocks and lost. As the ship settled down broadside to the shore, she gave some shelter from the raging seas. One man, John MacLeod, managed to swim ashore with a heaving line, and a hawser was hauled ashore and made fast to a rock. Some thirty to forty men climbed hand over hand along the rope and were saved.

As news of the disaster came through to the throngs of people waiting on the quayside, some made their way in the dark to Holm to search for survivors. Altogether, 75 men were saved.

It was a terrible disaster which shocked the world, and especially cruel for a small island like Lewis. Wives became widows, children were left without fathers. With every second home losing a member of their family, a generation was lost. It is only now I realise why my granny and grandfather's generation were all dressed in black, and why my parents' generation were so serious.

Some of the survivors from that disaster came from our own village. I actually went out on the fishing boat with John MacInnes, one of the survivors. I was not aware of this at the time as he never mentioned it in my presence. I was in my teens before I read about it. The story of the sinking of the *Iolaire* is told by John MacLeod in his excellent book *When I Heard the Bell.* Although there have been many disasters at sea involving Lewis sailors and fisherman, the sea is still in our blood and I was one of those who chose to follow it.

After the end of the First World War servicemen were promised crofts but this did not materialise, and there was a lot of unrest against the lairds who owned the land. In the case of my own village, Gress, people raided the farm and split the land into crofts, and this happened in other parts of the island. At the time Lewis was owned by Lord Leverhulme, the founder of Lever Brothers (now Unilever). He eventually gave the whole island to the people. There was still a lot of unemployment and many chose to emigrate. In 1923 and 1924, two ships, the *Metagama* and the *Marloch*, took over 400 men, women and children to Canada, and this so soon after the war left a greater void in that generation. My father, uncle and three aunties were among them. There is little wonder that those left behind were so sad.

Growing up on the Island

I had two brothers and two sisters. A family photo taken around 1945 gives a false impression, suggesting that our lives were not happy. We are all shown in a pretty sober mood. The four astronauts in the signed photo they gave me in 1969 look happier on their way to the moon than we do in that picture.

In fact, we lacked for nothing, although everything was still rationed. We caught sea fish off the rocks or from our boats, salmon and trout in the river and lochs. We were self-sufficient from the croft, with our own potatoes, our own vegetables and our own lamb. Every house had a cow which supplied us with milk, butter and crowdie, and we had our own hens and eggs. We had plenty of venison, although the landlord didn't know about it. We had no electricity. Light was by a paraffin tilley lamp or hand-held storm lamps for the barn. Peats were harvested in the springtime for heating. We had no running water. Water was fetched from the village well in pails. There was a community spirit, though, and everyone helped each other with spring planting, cutting and drying peats and in the autumn with the harvest. During the long winter evenings the elder statesmen met in different houses and we as children listened intently to their stories.

Eighty percent of the population of Lewis have a nickname. I don't know to this day how some of these (and they could be quite cruel) came to be applied. In our own village we had names like Pedro, Butch, Swannie, Kipper, Cake, Bread, Dondy, Sailor, Prize, Poshan and Bobshie. Others were known as Sandy Daft, Geordie Ugly and Kenny Deadly. In my own case I was christened 'Lemon' – for what reason I have no idea. A few weeks back from the time of writing this, a lad everyone knew as Tiddler was taken to hospital suffering from a heart attack. We were in a local club when we heard the news. One of us decided to telephone the hospital to see how he was getting on, and asked around as to what was Tiddler's proper name. We all looked at each other and shrugged our shoulders. Although we had known the guy for years we did not know his name was John MacLeod. I above all should have known this, because when I was in the drug squad I had him stopped and searched as he was coming into London Airport. I will tell that story later on.

Sanitation was a problem, although at the time I never gave it a second thought. During my childhood, sanitation progressed in three phases. In my earliest years one went to the toilet in the barn using the same trench as the cows used. The result was shovelled into a wheelbarrow every morning and emptied in the manure tip further down the croft.

The second phase was referred to as a dry lavvy (lavatory). Most householders had an outhouse, measuring about 4ft x 4ft, built to accommodate this new invention. It consisted of a large round drum with a toilet seat. This was a luxury compared with the squatting position. Our barn and byre were attached to the house, so we were lucky as we did not have to go outside. My father built a cubicle in the barn using sheets of plasterboard. It was easy to knock a tiny hole in it for my pal Butch and myself to spy on the occupant, especially if she was a friend of my sisters. The drawback was my poor mother had to empty out the drum when it was full.

In later years the 'coolies' in Egypt reminded me of this when they came aboard ship to load or unload cargo when we went through the Suez Canal. The first thing they did was to rig a box over the stern of the ship. This was called a 'thunder-box' and they used it as a toilet. They had one advantage over my mother, namely that they did not have to empty the contents, as whatever they did went straight into the Canal.

The third and most exciting phase was when we had a proper modern bathroom, fitted with a septic tank dug away from the house. Water was channelled from the roof into a large tank built at sufficient height for the water to be used for flushing the toilet by pressing the handle. This was indeed a luxury, and for the first time we were able to have a proper bath with running water.

Throughout these three phases we had no toilet paper. Newspapers like the *Stornoway Gazette*, *People's Friend* and the *Weekly News* (there were no daily papers) were cut into squares with hole made in one corner. A piece of string went through the sheets and they were hung on a nail. By the time our weekly bath came round I am sure one could read an article from the *People's Friend* off my bum.

The nearest telephone was three miles away. Television arrived some 30 years later. Ploughing was done by horse-power. I remember the last horse and the first tractor coming to the village.

Electricity came to the island around 1952, and poles for carrying the cables were erected. One of the most exciting games we played then was 'up the pole and down the stay', or 'up the stay and down the pole'. This was not for the faint-hearted, as the poles were quite high. Health and safety had not been heard of.

I had no English when I went to school; our language was Gaelic. School was three miles away and we had to walk there hail, rain or snow. We had few or no toys but we had plenty of open spaces for playing, sea and rivers to swim in, moorland to shoot over, machair to play football on and sand-dunes for playing cowboys and Indians. A piece of wood cut in the shape of a boat, with a pointed stem and square stern with a makeshift sail, was ideal for launching in the stream running down from our house.

For daredevil reasons we took a fancy to stealing certain villagers' carrots or turnips. Most vegetable plots were close to the house, and if we were detected a chase by the enraged crofter was a certainty. This was what gave us a thrill. Another ploy we had during the long winter evening was knocking on the windows of households where someone lived who we were certain would give us a run for our money. A chase could go right round the village in complete darkness. This was where one required forward planning. Before the actual knocking took place, we worked out a route for the chase and a hiding place should the crofter get too close on our tail. I still laugh to myself at these silly but enjoyable pranks. My children and grandchildren don't believe me when I tell them what our pastimes were in my younger days.

A couple of years ago the local schoolmaster asked me to give the children a talk on my childhood days. I dressed up in short baggy trousers, an old pair of tackety boots, and ran into the classroom with a bicycle wheel at the end of a length of wire which went through the hole in the axle. This was one of our favourite toys. As children we would run all over the village pretending the wheel was a lorry: one '*Brrrrr*' would double the clutch, then more '*Brrrrrs*' would sound as we progressed through second, third and top gear. We would call at every house, pretending that we were taking home their peats, reversing into the front of their doors and tipping the imaginary load of peats at their doorstep. Our imaginary lorry even went into the ditch. We would have one foot in a ditch and the other on the road. We had to wait in this lopsided position until the next child arrived with another load and gave us an imaginary tow. It was a great pastime. The children I was giving the talk to were mesmerised, and just looked at me with their mouths open.

Another toy we made for ourselves was a tractor. This was made out of a cotton reel. Notches were made around both ends to make it look like the spikes on the iron wheels of the Fordson tractors that were commonly used in those days. An elastic band was put through the hole in the middle of the reel. A matchstick or a small nail was tied to one end to stop the elastic coming through, and at the other end was a thin slice cut from a candle with a hole through the middle. The elastic went into the hole and then a pencil or something similar was put through this end and the elastic was wound tight. When it was tight enough the contraption was put on the floor, and the elastic unwinding itself propelled the cotton reel. The notches in the wheel allowed the reel to climb over any small obstacle that it encountered.

During the evenings boys and girls from surrounding villages gathered on the road by the old mill. Some of the boys had melodeons and soon a ceilidh/dance would be in full swing, complete with eightsome reels, Dashing White Sergeant, and military two-steps. Should a young damsel be feeling fruity, a crossbar ride on the bike to the sand dunes was likely, where we played doctors and nurses!

Saturday evening was bath night. Water was fetched from the well and boiled on the stove. A large zinc bath was taken into the kitchen and that was where all the children had their weekly bath.

Saturday night was spent preparing for church on Sunday. Shoes had to be polished, Sunday broth and dinner were prepared and bibles left ready on the table. We walked three miles to church and three miles back in the morning and the same again in the evening. Children only attended the evening service.

Around 1950 a bus service started. Many of the churchgoers refused to pay the bus driver on a Sunday but would pay him on the Monday morning. The reason for this was the bus driver was working on the Sunday and they believed Sunday was supposed to be a day of rest.

Others refused to use the bus at all, and carried on walking the six miles in the morning and the same to the evening service. In later years, as families got richer, some purchased their own vehicles. The ones who refused to go on the bus would travel in a car belonging to the family, and for some unknown reason they found nothing wrong with this. Sunday was not a good day for a boisterous kid. Sweets were still on ration, and Sunday was a day for candy-making once our parents went to church. Candy made on the open fire was a great treat, but one had to be careful, as sugar was also rationed and mother would soon find out if we used too much.

One of our saddest days in school was on 22 July 1953, when two sisters, Bella and Jean Ferguson, were drowned in the local river. Bella used to sit beside me in school. It was a terrible disaster to happen anywhere, but I think more so in such a small village where everyone knew each other.

I was 15 before I crossed the Minch to mainland Scotland. My friend Murdo 'Butch' MacKenzie was born in Glasgow, and was about four years old when the family returned to live in our village. He had obviously seen a train and was forever winding me up about the fact that I was two years older than him and still had not seen one.

This particular evening he decided to give me a demonstration as to how a train travelled. We both got on our bikes at the top of a hill on the main road through the village. It was a pitch black night. Butch had a torch on his bike while I had no light at all, but off we went, both of us pedalling like hell. I could hear Butch going '*choo, choo – choo, choo – choo choo*', pretending to be the Kyle of Lochalsh to Glasgow steam train. I had travelled about 500 yards when I went flying over the handlebars for no apparent reason.

When I got up to retrieve my bike, I stumbled over a human body. I was absolutely petrified. I had knocked over an old lady from the village. Along with her sister-in-law, they were on their way to the prayer meeting. Every lady on the island in these days used to dress in black, so I suppose to a certain extent one could say she was camouflaged.

Mrs Morrison was severely injured and suffered a fractured skull. Fortunately for me she made a full recovery, and lived to an even older age. Butch and I were prosecuted, Butch for having no rear light and me for having no lights at all. We subsequently appeared at Stornoway Sheriff Court, where we pleaded guilty. I was fined £5.00 and Butch 10/- (ten shillings). As we had no proper shoes to wear for our court appearance, I had to borrow my uncle's brogues. The toecaps were stuffed with newspaper so they would fit me. Butch was in the same position and had to wear his grandmother's Sunday boots. Years later I had to ask Dan MacKenzie, the village constable who prosecuted us, for a reference when I joined the Met. He gave me an excellent reference and made no mention of the above incident.

My grandfather's house was next door to us, and my uncle Colin lived there. Colin had a bus and a lorry. They also had the agency for selling paraffin. There were three Harris tweed weaving looms in the shed, which were operated by ex-servicemen who had just been de-mobbed. The loom-shed was the hub of the village, and I spent most of my childhood days around there listening to the men's experiences in the Merchant Navy, Army and Air Force. I remember one of them was on HMS *Fiji* and his brother was on HMS *Illustrious* when they were torpedoed in the Mediterranean. I was enthralled by stories of D-Day landings, of U-boats sinking merchant ships and planes shot down. Harris tweed weaving and fishing were the main industries on the island after the war. Every second house in the village had a loom, but, sadly, today there are none.

It was in one of the loom-sheds I saw my first pair of boxing gloves, and it was there I had my first boxing lesson. These were exciting times for a five-year-old. I am afraid I also learnt at that early age some tasty vocabulary. One day I was watching some ex-servicemen playing football on the machair. One of them, who in later years I sailed with, was fouled by an opponent and he called him a 'whore'. I remember coming home that day and using this newly acquired word 'whore' to my mother. Mother didn't have a clue what the word meant. Somehow she found out and the following day she told me if I ever used that word again she would wash my mouth out with soap. The slices of red carbolic soap did not appeal to me, and I never used the word again until my days in the merchant navy when I first came across a real one in Glasgow. I will mention her later.

One of my proudest moments was when I was given an old navy cap that one of the men had worn during hostilities. I wore that cap for ages with the chin strap shortened to fit.

I attended the local secondary school to the age of 15. I was never top of the class and I was never bottom. I did reasonably well in most subjects, apart from religion and algebra. In Sunday school an old elder from the church who was our teacher asked me, 'Who was the first murderer?' I told him 'My brother', as he had bullied me as a child. I remember the headmaster marking my algebra paper and giving me a mark of 3 because he felt sorry for me and I had spelled my name right. I did better than my classmate who got zero, as he had spelled his name as Agnes instead of Angus. I can never remember doing any homework. I got to school early most days and targeted the studious girls who I knew would have done their homework and copied the answers from them.

As soon as school closed for the day I was out to meet the fishing boats or going out on the boat or doing the fish-round with my cousin, who was the local fish cadger. Another hobby was ploughing the crofts with the local tractor. Dondy, the owner, always allowed me to drive his tractor.

I learned to drive on my uncle's Bedford square-nose ex-army truck. By the age of 12 or 13 I was a competent driver, and I am sure would have easily passed my driving test. In the early 50s there were very few cars in the surrounding villages. They were all pre-war models and did not have ignition keys. Every Thursday evening there was a prayer meeting in the church and a few of those attending the meeting had cars. I remember a Hillman, a Morris 8 and an Austin 16. They were parked by the roadside while their owners were in church. Street lights were unheard of, and with no ignition key needed to start them it was a great temptation for an experienced driver like me. I have to plead guilty to 'taking and driving away' some of the cars on several occasions, driving them round the village, then placing them back in their original positions before the prayer meeting ended. Some of my classmates, many of them elders in the church today, enjoyed these joyrides.

The Hebrides are famous for their staunch religious beliefs and heavy drinking. These go hand in hand. When the islanders have had too much drink over too long a period and are recovering from DTs they turn to religion, and when they turn to religion they become a pain in the ass. I will mention more on religion later.

Although I was brought up at a time when food was rationed, fish, especially the silver darlings, herring, was available in abundance. Stornoway was then one of the main ports for landing herring. In fact the first canned herring ever was produced in Stornoway by Lord Leverhulme, who owned the island after the First World War. Stornoway kippers were famous. Sadly, all this has disappeared and the port is no longer classed as a fish-landing port.

The community spirit in the village was something I will always remember. Everyone helped each other. After the work was done there would be a ceilidh in someone's house. This community spirit has gone forever. All the crofts in the village lie dormant. I have to agree it is far easier nowadays to buy from the supermarket and at the touch of a switch have the house centrally heated than to return to the backbreaking croft work. Television has taken over. The neighbours now use the telephone to have a chat instead of visiting, and I can go weeks without talking to a neighbour. A wave as they pass in their 4x4 is the closest we get to each other.

Starting Work

I left school on a Friday and started work on the Monday as a van-boy on a grocery van and we travelled round the island. The van was owned by a local man, and we were in competition with the likes of the Co-op and Lipton, who were national companies and had been around for years. My boss was ahead of his time. His vans were fitted out with the first formica shelves and glass cabinets and were spotless. Our two competitors took their customers for granted, but very soon they withdrew their vans as all their customers had changed to the better and cleaner service we provided. I have never been unemployed since.

I was still 15 when I went to mainland Scotland to work alongside my father in building. The work was part of the hydroelectric schemes that were scattered all over Scotland at the time. This was the first time I had been to the mainland and the first time I had seen a train. I got a job with Carmichaels at Glascarnoch camp by Aultguish on the Ullapool road. We were building a tunnel to take water five miles through the mountains to a generator. Another company built the dam further down the valley. The Aultguish Inn was, and still is, next door to it. This dam was nicknamed 'The Whisky Dam', because there were so many empty whisky bottles thrown into the aggregate. Hydroelectric work was at that time equivalent to what North Sea oil exploration is now. The work was hard but the money was good, with plenty of overtime. These Hydro schemes were a fantastic feat of engineering, with huge dams and tunnels constructed throughout the Highland region.

Although we were only about 60 miles from home we were only able to get across the Minch every three months. It amazes me now when young men employed on North Sea oil rigs complain when they only do two weeks on and two weeks off.

Labour mostly came from the Highlands and Islands, but there was a large contingent of Irish labourers who lived a very rough life. They worked hard and played hard. On a Saturday they would travel to Dingwall or Inverness to buy a new suit. Saturday night was a heavy drinking and fighting session. On Sunday they would return to camp and collapse on the bed still wearing their new suits. On Monday morning they would be off to work still wearing the suit, and wore it without taking it off until the next Saturday, when they would repeat what they did the previous weekend. The suit was their dress suit, pyjamas and dungarees. They went to bed in their wellington boots. Heating in their accommodation was provided by a small stove in the middle of the room, and the smell of sweat and stale breath was overwhelming.

I never got on with my father. I can never remember him giving me a cuddle or praising me for anything I did. He was mostly away on the mainland working. I was quite pleased to see him leave and go back to the mainland when he had been home. Needless to say I didn't last long working with him.

2
Merchant Navy

In April 1957 I left to join the Merchant Navy. I was wearing a suit my father had bought for himself in Canada when he emigrated there in the 1920s. My suitcase was the size of a modern-day briefcase. Mum gave me £20 and off I went. I had a certificate from a local fishing skipper to say I had been a deck-hand on his boat the *Renown* for the past six months. I was told this should qualify me to sign on as a 'junior ordinary seaman'. In fact, I had never even seen the *Renown*, never mind sailed on her. This was at a time when Britain had a merchant fleet that was second to none. Nearly all able-bodied men on the island were seamen – an illustration of this is that there were 18 men from my own village leaving to go sailing that night.

We arrived in Glasgow on Saturday morning. The first problem I had was understanding the Glasgow accent. In the afternoon some of the girls from the village who were working in Glasgow took three of us 'first-timers' to Ibrox to see Rangers playing. This was my first time at a professional football match. On Saturday night I followed the adults and walked with them under the railway bridge in Argyle Street. The area of Argyle Street below this bridge was known as 'The Hielanman's Umbrella'. Everyone, and I mean everyone, in sight came from the Highlands or Islands, and everybody spoke Gaelic.

Dick's Bar on the Broomielaw was a pretty rough pub in a pretty rough area. I followed the adults to this pub. The place was full of island seamen. Gaelic was the language spoken amongst them. I had occasion to go to the toilet and was aware that another man had followed me. This man immediately threatened me and demanded money. I was pretty scared and gave him a ten-shilling note. By this time I had about £15 left of the original £20 my mother had given me. When I got out of the toilets to tell my mates, the bastard had vanished. This was my first taste of crime.

Going to Sea for the First Time

On Monday morning it was time to go to the Shipping Federation to look for a ship. I was accompanied by another first-tripper, Donald John MacDonald, who was also from our village. The officer behind the counter asked me, 'Where do you want to go, Sonny Jim?' I told him in my Hebridean English I wanted to go and see my uncle in Vancouver. 'Right,' he said, 'just the job for you here, sign on that dotted line.' I showed him the reference I had from the skipper of the *Renown*, which he ignored. I did as I was told and was absolutely delighted to be on my way to Vancouver. My ambition to sail as a junior ordinary seaman was dashed, however, when I found that I had signed on as a deck boy.

I told my mate Donald Iain, who was with me, that I was on my way to Vancouver. He agreed to come with me if there was another vacancy on the ship. Sure enough there was. He also signed on, and away we went to board our first ship, the *Merchant Prince*, an old tramp steamer.

Neither Donald nor myself had questioned the destination of our ship, and took it for granted what I had been told was true. The nearest telephone to our house in Lewis was about two miles away. Donald Iain's family were even further away from a telephone, so the only way we could tell them we had signed on a ship was by letter.

That night the two of us headed to Dick's Bar to tell our friends that we had signed on a ship. We were walking up the Broomielaw when a middle-aged woman came out of a close. The dock area in Glasgow was pretty rough in those days. This woman walked in front of us and said, 'Fiver for a short time'. I didn't have a clue what she was on about. I forgot I was in

Glasgow and naturally spoke to her in my native Gaelic. I said '*Deidh a tha thu a' gradh?*' ('What are you saying?'). She then said 'Fiver for a knee-trembler.' Donald Iain was as green as me and just said 'Whaaat?' The lady made an about-turn and we heard her mumbling 'You must be a couple of young teuchters [i.e. Highlanders].' When we got to Dick's Bar we told older sailors what the woman had said. They creased up laughing. For some reason unknown to us at the time, they all knew exactly who the lady of the night was – 'Irish Nelly', who they told us was a whore. After all these years I had finally found out what a whore was. The boys explained she wanted a fiver to pay to have sex with her. No wonder my mother was angry!

We set sail down the Clyde the following day. There were two seasoned ABs (able-bodied seamen) on board from the Isle of Lewis. On the second day out I asked one of them, 'How long will it take to get to Vancouver?' 'Vancouver?' he replied, 'What makes you think we are going to Vancouver?' I told him the man at the Shipping Federation told me the ship was going there, and he couldn't stop laughing. We were actually heading for West Africa via Las Palmas.

I was fair-skinned, freckled, with a fair complexion and ginger hair, and exposing my body to the sun was not a good idea. As we were steaming through the tropics I, like everyone else, stripped off and sunbathed. By the end of the day one would have thought I had been barbecued. I was ill for a week. Unknown to me getting sunburnt was a disciplinary offence, but I was so ill the Captain didn't take any action against me.

Sailing round the West African coast was an eye-opener. Our first port of call was Las Palmas for bunkers (i.e. oil), then we sailed down the coast via Dakar, Freetown, Sapele, Accra and Lagos. All these places were very primitive. As we approached the coast, waiting for a pilot, about 10 canoes paddled like hell towards the ship. The first one to come alongside was the pilot who navigated the ship into port. He was followed by more canoes known as 'bum-boats' selling their wares. The women were shouting up at us, 'You dash we flash'. This meant if we threw coins into the water they would flash their tits whilst the men dived for the coins. I spent a week's wage in a couple of minutes!

Sapele is an outpost up a long winding river and in the middle of the jungle. We were anchored in the middle of the river with ropes attached to trees on the bank. The way this was done was that some of the natives swam to the ship, carrying a heaving line in their mouth, swam back and tied the attached hawser to trees. We were taken ashore by local tribesmen in canoes. The captain advised us not to go ashore, as the previous evening two Norwegians had been beheaded and eaten by cannibals! Our cargo of logs was floated out to the ship and lifted on board by the ship's derricks. We also loaded bags of cocoa beans.

The heat in the jungle was unbelievable, and to cool off during the day we used to swim out to the logs that were in the river waiting to be loaded. I was never a good swimmer, but because it was so hot I decided to follow suit and swim with the rest of the seamen. I took on more than I could chew. I failed to reach one of the logs and panicked. I went under and could see the propeller of the ship above me. I was saved by an AB who had seen me going down. Once again I learned a lesson the hard way.

On the way out from Sapele we were in collision with a Palm Line ship. She hit us on the boat deck, or we may have hit her – I don't remember who was to blame. However, we lost all the lifeboats on one side, but carried on anyway to Rotterdam where we were paid off. The rest of the journey to London was by train and ferry.

Other Voyages

My next ship was the *Rangitiki* owned by the New Zealand Shipping Company. Seventy percent of the deck hands came from the Hebrides. We picked her up from Harland and Wolff dry dock in Belfast where she had an overhaul. The Rangi boats, *Rangitiki*, *Rangitoto*, *Rangitani* and *Rangitata* were famous during the war as troop-carriers. John Prescott, who went on to be Deputy Prime Minister, was a steward on these ships and on Cunard Line ships. The *Rangitiki* was a cargo/passenger boat sailing on a regular basis to New Zealand and back to the UK. Outward bound we usually had a cargo of heavy plant and machinery and returned with lamb and fruit.

Each trip lasted between four and five months. The voyage was via the Panama Canal with a stop at the Pitcairn Islands to deliver and pick up mail. We sailed for five to six weeks round the New Zealand coast, calling in at various ports. There was a shortage of stevedores in New Zealand at the time, so after we finished our day's work on board our ship we went to work with the stevedores. For this we were paid New Zealand hourly rates, which were much higher than our usual rate. On our return to the UK I was paid off in London.

My next ship was the *Hertford*, a Federal Steam Ship freighter. Everyone on deck came from the Hebrides apart from the little deck boy who came from London. The bosun, Roddy Mackinnon (Ruaridh Mor), came from Barra, Angus MacAskill came from the isle of Eriskay and all the ABs came from Lewis, Uist and Barra. I did two trips on her. Our first trip was to New Zealand via the Panama Canal. The captain's name was Smythe. He was about 5ft 6in and had very little sense of humour. When we got to Panama I was standing by the rope ladder waiting to give the pilot a hand with his bag. The captain was standing beside me waiting to welcome the pilot on board. As the pilot came up the ladder and on to the deck he was welcomed on board by our captain. 'Good morning, Captain Smith,' said the pilot.

Our captain replied, 'My name is not Smith, my name is Smythe.'

'Smith or Smythe, shit or shite, all the same here, mate,' said the Yankee pilot.

Our captain did not appreciate being spoken to like that in front of one of his most junior crew members.

My second trip on the *Hertford* was to Australia via the Suez Canal. Once again all the seamen on deck apart from the London deck boy came from the islands. A couple of days before we sailed, my oldest sister got married in Inverness. I just made it to the wedding. My sister gave me a bottle of whisky to give to my aunty Chrissie in Adelaide. My friend and I drank the bottle before we got to Perth.

We called at most seaports in Aussie: Fremantle, Adelaide, Melbourne, Sydney, Townsville and Hobart in Tasmania. I remember being in the Wallamalloo Pub in Sydney. The barman came round with a hat, asking us seamen to pick out a numbered ticket. The numbers referred to a line of prostitutes. The one I picked out was a huge Aborigine woman, and I gracefully declined – that's what I say.

In December 1958 I was again in London. Funds were low so I wanted to ship out before New Year. On 30 December I met John MacDonald, another islander, affectionately known as 'Scroobie'. We went down to the Shipping Federation looking for a ship and we were offered the SS *Gothic*, a Shaw Savill cargo/passenger boat. In 1953 the *Gothic* had taken the Queen on a world tour. A lot of seamen refused to sail on her, as they were afraid of her Royalty connection and thought that there would be too much discipline. When the shipping officer told us there was a vacancy on the *Gothic*, Scroobie replied, 'If she is good enough for the Queen she is good enough for us'. We sailed for New Zealand on New Year's Day 1958. This was my fourth trip to New Zealand and Australia and I was still only 17. Sadly, John was killed in a road traffic accident in Melbourne while assigned to another ship.

One extremely hot afternoon we were berthed in Lyttelton, New Zealand. Scroobie and I were painting the hull of the ship from the wharf. As usual we were both skint and dying for a pint. As it came to dinnertime two of the ship's stewards, whom we knew to be homosexual, passed us on their way to the pub. They asked us to join them, but we told them we were financially embarrassed. 'Never mind,' they said, 'we have a few bob.' We decided to take them up on their offer.

The paint and the rollers were left on the quayside and off we went with them. We stayed ashore until after closing time, which in those days in New Zealand was 6 pm. We were both a little under the weather as we returned, and the captain and the mate were on the bridge watching us. The following morning our bosun told us the captain wanted a word. We were both a bit sheepish in front of him, especially as he had seen us with the two stewards. He 'logged' us (i.e. fined us) ten shillings for going AWOL. I still have the piece of paper he served on us outlining the case against us. As we left the cabin with our tails down he said, 'I was surprised at the company you keep'. We took some ribbing from the rest of the ABs. This was the first and last time I was fined as a seaman.

The *Colorado Star* was a Blue Star ship running to the West Coast of the United States and Canada. She carried a cargo of whisky which we loaded in Glasgow and Liverpool. Glasgow dockers knew how to broach the barrels of pure spirit. I have never seen so much whisky. Every kettle, sauce bottle, tea-pot, bucket and any other vessel capable of holding liquid were filled with whisky. Every time we entered and left a port the ropes had to be stored in the hold, and every time this was done, up came half a dozen cases of whisky.

Once again I went through the Panama Canal and up the west coast of the States, calling in at San Francisco, Los Angeles, Portland Oregon, Seattle, Vancouver and Vancouver Island. Two years after I sailed from Glasgow on my first trip I eventually got to Vancouver! I well remember my first dinner in my uncle's house. The starter was corn on the cob. I had never seen this vegetable and had no idea how to eat it. He was well aware of this, and when I attacked it with a knife and fork everyone burst into laughter.

In San Francisco I was put on the job of chipping rust with the electric chipping machine. It was a dirty filthy job. The dust stuck on your sweating body and a lot of it was inhaled. No masks were issued in those days. You got very, very thirsty through swallowing the dust from the rust. The weather was good and we were all in shorts. I decided to go for a beer in the nearest pub on the waterfront before having a shower.

In those days our issue of cigarettes came in round tins, each tin containing 50 cigarettes. The tin was bulky, too bulky really to have in your pocket, so everyone carried a slim cigarette case that you transferred the cigarettes into. On this occasion, as I was only going for a quick beer, I just slipped the round tin of Woodbines into my pocket.

As I was sitting by the bar I took the tin out to have a fag and left it on the bar. I noticed that the attention of a lady sitting not far away was attracted to the tin.

I was happy enough to attract her attention, but not so happy with the filthy state I was in. Anyway, after a while she came over and said, 'Gee, I've never seen cigarettes in a tin like that. Are you English?'

I said, 'No, darling, I'm Scots. Take a few cigarettes. Actually you can have the tin, I have plenty on board ship. Please excuse my state of dress. I'm just going back on board for a shower.'

'Are you a real sailor?' she replied, 'can I buy you a drink?'

I said, 'No, thanks. I am financially embarrassed, and everything is so expensive in the States.'

'Sailor, don't worry about that,' she replied, 'I would love to buy a young Scotsman a drink. I suppose you'll have "Scotch on the rocks".'

I didn't have a clue what she meant by this, but readily agreed to accept her offer. She bought me a drink which I thought was whisky with ice. When I tasted it I asked the barman what blend of whisky it was, and he told me it was Japanese *sake*. 'Good enough for me,' I thought.

The problem was, she couldn't stop buying, and after about the sixth or seventh I wanted to go back on board for a shower and something to eat. 'Don't worry about that,' she told me. 'I'll drive you back to the ship, you can have a shower and I'll take you out for a meal.'

This was the first time I realised she had a car, and what a car! It was a huge American model with the boot longer than the engine. We finished our drinks and she staggered out to the car. I jumped in the passenger seat and we headed towards my ship. Now the fun began. All docks have a railway line for the cargo to be loaded or unloaded on the ships. There are also level crossings at various points for vehicles to cross. When we got closer to my ship I told her to take the next level crossing, which she missed by about 20 feet. The front wheels went over the railway line and the car was stuck resting on the chassis with the rear wheels spinning in the air. She kept revving the engine until I eventually managed to switch it off. I got out and told her I would get some assistance. I told the first dock worker I saw, who went over to her. I crept away back to my ship, feeling sorry for her, as I think she really was going to look after me!

I did two trips on the *Colorado Star.* She was a really happy ship, and I would have stayed on her but my liver couldn't take any more whisky.

I signed on the *Imperial Star* on 21 December 1959. We went into dry dock in Swansea where we stayed over the Christmas and New Year period with a skeleton crew. We had no heating and the accommodation was freezing. On Christmas Eve the other two ABs and me went ashore for a few beers. We were not in the bar for long when we pulled three lovely ladies. We invited them back to the ship for a few festive drinks. As the party was gathering pace, everyone was merry and getting to know each other, if you know what I mean.

One of the Cockney ABs came back from the toilet and pulled me to one side. He said, 'Jock, have you had your hand up her yet?'

I said, 'Give us a chance . . . there's plenty time. Why do you ask?'

He said, 'Well, that's the first time I ever saw a woman pissing in the men's urinal.'

I was dumbstruck and replied, 'What about yours, have you had a feel?'

'No, but I am just about to,' he said, and off he went with his lady. A couple of minutes later Phil, the other AB, came back into the mess room laughing his head off, saying, 'My bitch is the same!' Needless to say, the 'ladies' were given a quick escort off the ship. I was quite relieved that all three were of the same gender and not just mine, as I would have never lived it down.

I did another trip to Australia on the *Imperial Star*. Two days out of Melbourne I fell from a derrick and was sure my wrist was broken. When we got to Aden this was confirmed. By that time it had healed at a terrible angle and has never been right since.

I did several more trips on various ships to the Mediterranean and finally left the Merchant Navy in 1960.

3

Whaling Years

Christian Salvesen and Son in my time was a household name in the Outer Hebrides and Shetland, as they employed hundreds of islanders as whalers. The Salvesen family originally came from Norway, where they were involved with shipping, based in the small town of Mandal. Around 1871 Christian Salvesen opened an office in Leith, Scotland. Salvesen and Co. branched into the whaling industry, first in the Arctic, and in 1907 they sent a ship, the *Coronda,* to the Falkland Islands and fished for whales there. A year later the company moved further south and founded the whaling station Leith Harbour in South Georgia. This station fished continuously, apart from the war years, until it closed in 1961. The history of Salvesen's whaling days is fully documented in an excellent book written by Sir Gerald Elliot (*A Whaling Enterprise*). Salvesen employed 60% Norwegian workers and 40% British. The British contingent mostly came from the Shetlands, the Western Isles, Edinburgh, Dundee and Tyneside.

There was a whaling station fishing from Harris on the Outer Hebrides for about 18 seasons between 1904 and up to 1951 under Norwegian and British management. It was based near Tarbet at Bunavoneader. The ruins remain the last vestiges of a modern whaling station anywhere in the United Kingdom. The factory chimney-stack and the plan-deck area together with a few outhouses still remain.

During the summer of 1960 I was home on leave from the Merchant Navy. Local whalers were getting ready to leave for the 1960 whaling expedition down to the Antarctic. At that time there were 40 houses in my village and 20 whalers from there. While I enjoyed every minute of my Merchant Navy days, I suppose one could say I enjoyed it too much. The fact is that in the three years I was in the Merchant Navy I never saved a penny. I decided to follow the rest of the whalers and try and seek employment with Salvesen. My intention was to overwinter in South Georgia. This would give me a chance to save some money.

I must stress I didn't go whaling simply because I wanted to kill whales. It just happened and I followed the crowd. It was just another job for us in those days. I can now say I am not in favour of killing these beautiful mammals.

All whalers headed for Leith, to Salvesen's office in Bernard Street. Leith was then a thriving seaport, and was much more so when the whalers arrived in town. Every whaler knew he was going to be away for at least nine months or two years, so one could not blame them for being a bit boisterous. The publicans, prostitutes, pimps, police and priests certainly had their hands full. The ladies of the night must have made a fortune. As a good-living Wee Free Protestant myself I can say I never went to see the priest to confess any misdemeanour, but that does not mean to say I was innocent.

The men who had previously sailed with Salvesen on previous seasons had already got a job, but first-trippers like me had to queue up morning and afternoon and wait for a vacancy. Once a vacancy was confirmed one was then sent for a medical. Dr Iain MacIntosh came from Harris in the Hebrides. Old Mac, as he was affectionately known, would ask you to bend down. He would have a quick peep up your backside, then ask you to cough. You were then certified fit to spend the next two years in Antarctica. Had anyone medically examined Old Mac himself I am sure he would have without question failed the medical. He was a chain-smoker who coughed a lot, and he loved his dram.

A seasoned whaler from Stornoway, Norman MacDonald, told me one of his mates had a bad cold. He went to see Old Mac and asked if he could have medicine to cure it. Mac gave his advice: 'Yes, go and buy a bottle of rum, two oranges and a glass. Place an orange on both the bottom bedposts. Keep sipping the rum until you see three oranges, and then you should be cured.'

Another whaler went to see Old Mac as he had pain in his stomach. Mac gave him four pills. He told him to take two before he went to bed, and if he was alive the following morning, to take the other two.

Needless to say, the last night in Leith was pretty hectic or should I say 'heady', with sore heads galore the next day. Tam Gordon, in his book *Whaling Thoughts Recalled*, describes one of his mates, Dougie MacDonald, a Gaelic-speaking Heilanman saying to him, 'Do you know, Tommy, this morning both my mouths were stuck together with the dry.' Dougie, of course, meant his two lips were stuck together. I think this was an excellent statement of how most of us felt.

The day I found out I had a job as a whaler I met my cousin who was doing his National Service in Redford Barracks. We met a character from Lewis who was living in Leith. He had a Ford V8 Pilot car, a very posh vehicle in those days. He suggested we go to a dance in Glasgow.

We were joined by another straggler, Roddy Morrison, who was also on his way to the Antarctic. We arrived in Glasgow without any hitches and parked the car as close as we could to the Overnewton dance hall. We had a great time and, as one can imagine, a good drink. This would be our last dance for a couple of years. When the dancing was over we went to find our car, but it was nowhere in sight despite what we thought was a really thorough search. We reported the theft to a couple of patrolling policemen. The first question they asked was, 'Where did you leave it?' We looked at one another and all of us shrugged our shoulders and couldn't give an answer. The officers told us to come back when we were in a position to say where the car was stolen from. Suffice to say, the car was parked exactly where we left it.

On the way back to Leith I fell asleep in the back seat. I woke up to the sound of a police car bell ringing alongside us. Our bold driver had driven the wrong way up Leith Walk, which was a one-way street. We were all arrested and taken to the cop shop. The driver was charged accordingly and I have never seen him since. That was my last memory of Leith – being dragged into the police station.

Going Whaling

The following day we were ushered to waiting buses and driven down to Falmouth on the south coast of England, some 450 miles away. Our luggage was loaded into trucks that accompanied the convoy. There was no room on the buses for luggage, as we were all laden with 'carry-outs' to quench our thirst on the long journey south. And it was a long, long journey. There was no motorway service stations in those days, and no toilets in the bus. Had the driver stopped every time a whaler wanted a pee the bus would still be on the road. You just opened the bus door and poured forth, only to get it all back in your face. Talk about 'pissing in the wind'.

On arrival in Falmouth we boarded the *Southern Opal*, a converted tanker with accommodation for roughly 200 whalers. She was built in 1941 and was well past her sell-by date in 1960. On a good day she would do eight knots, but she did not have many good days. Our first and last port of call was Las Palmas. For many of us this was our last taste of civilisation for twenty months.

Las Palmas is famous for large lifelike dolls. I bought one for my then only niece and had to guard her desperately from some of the randy whalers. Las Palmas is also famous for rum. The particular brand we bought was the cheapest. The label on the bottle had the face of a black woman, and she gave you the biggest hangover ever.

It was a leisurely trip down with very little to do apart from chipping rust with the dreaded chipping machine, scraping and painting. The deck had to be covered with wood ready for the whales to be hauled on board. This was, as I later found out, a necessary task. When the whaling season started, if the deck was left with the steel surface exposed it would be impossible to walk on it with the slippery whale oil.

We docked in Leith Harbour, South Georgia, during the early hours. I looked out the porthole and was faced with the side of a mountain covered in ice and snow. This mountain was known to all whalers as Coronda Peak. Captain Cook, who gave South Georgia its name when he discovered it in 1775, described the islands as:

> Lands doomed by nature to perpetual frigidness; never to feel the warmth of the sun's rays; whose horrible and savage aspect I have no words to describe.

These were certainly not encouraging words to the young Highlanders who over six decades braved the elements to earn the mythical fortunes provided by 'the whaling'. However, after several weeks at sea it was good to see land. Leith Harbour was quite a thriving settlement, with several barracks for accommodation and mess-rooms, as well as corrugated iron buildings housing the boiler-room, blacksmith, engineering workshop, factory buildings and a piggery. The manager had a large villa with his office next door. It looked like any industrial settlement on mainland Britain.

Once we docked in Leith Harbour we were welcomed by the boys who had overwintered. Most of them had full beards, and although many were friends from home, one did not recognise them unless they actually introduced themselves. Letters were delivered from loved ones and the latest gossip from home was exchanged. A few bottles of 'the black lady' from Las Palmas were made available and shared between everyone. That first day was a day to remember.

Within a few hours it was explained to me what a 'brew' was. This was a method of making home-brewed booze. A brew was made up of a few gallons of water in a metal drum, with yeast, sugar and possibly fruit or raisins, if available, added. The mixture was then allowed to ferment for up to 14 days. When it was ready it was then stilled. Some whalers did not have the patience to wait for the brew to ferment properly and drank the liquid as it was. They were easily identified as they burped throughout the day. The brew was still fermenting inside their stomachs.

The day we arrived I was invited by a whaler who had over-wintered to accompany him. He lifted a trap door that led us under the foundation of the building, and by the light of a candle I was shown my first home-made still. My friend Poshan MacIver explained to me how it worked. A metal drum of the kind used for storing the 'meat extract' from the whale was fitted with a kettle element. The brew, when it was ready, was poured into this drum and sealed. It was then heated to boiling point, producing steam that went through a pipe in the lid, which in turn passed through a cooler filled with cold water. The steam turned into liquid and the end result was alcohol. It dripped out of the end of the cooler into a waiting bottle. Every few minutes the spirit was tested to see if it was of good quality. The method we used for testing was to let a few drops fall onto a piece of wood then set it alight. If the flame was blue it was good; if it was turning yellow the spirit was getting poisonous. A good brew would produce normally about seven bottles of spirit. This in turn was diluted with cold tea or burnt sugar. The end product looked and tasted as good as real whisky, or so I thought.

I was pretty dizzy from the fumes coming from the still in such a cramped space and when we finished and came up to the room above we started drinking it. A couple of hours later I was so sick I thought I was going to die. I had an empty stomach with nothing to come up. I sat in the toilet and all I could think of was what was my mother going to say if she found out I had died from alcoholic poisoning and been buried in the ice in South Georgia. However, the following morning I was as right as rain.

The Whaling Season

The fishing season for the island started on 1 October. From then on all the activity was around the plan-deck, a large area of about an acre and covered with wood. It slopped towards the sea. The whale was delivered from the catcher and moored to a buoy, then towed over to the plan-deck by motor boat. A wire strap was put round the tail of the whale. It was then hauled by winch up on to the deck where the lemmers and flensers were waiting, armed with flensing knives, which had a four-foot-long handle.

Any butcher would be proud of the skills those men had. The knife was inserted into the whale behind the head, and as it was dragged up the plan-deck by wire and winch, they stood still with the knife in the whale and let the winch do the work. Then the blubber was cut away and disposed of in a kettle. The real butchering then began. All the different parts of the whale were sent to different plants to be boiled and the oil extracted. The backbone was cut out and hauled onto the bone-loft, where a steam-saw cut it up into portions small enough to go into the kettles. The jawbone also went to a large steam-saw where it was cut up too. The meat went to what was called the 'rosedown', where it was cut into lumps about two feet square, small enough to go into the kettle. The tongue, with the intestines and the heart, went to the 'hartman'. This was where I worked. The liver went to a special plant where the oil was separated from it. Liver oil was of the highest quality and worth a lot of money.

Every whaler working on the plan-deck had to wear leather boots with spiked heels. Oil and blood from the whale made it impossible to walk in ordinary boots. The leather boots came up to the knee. Canvas leggings were sewn onto the top of the boot, to stop the blood from getting into our boots. These leggings came up to the waist. As a 'hooker' on the hartman, without any exaggeration I was most of the time up to my belly in blood and guts.

My job was to pull a winch wire and place it round the intestines. These were then heaved up on a derrick and cut into a large bucket, which took them up to another floor and emptied them into a kettle for boiling. The same process was carried out with the tongue. The tongue was left attached to what was called the 'belly speck'. It was impossible to stand on the tongue as it rolled underneath your feet like mercury. This was the reason it was left attached to a bit of blubber from the belly. It was hoisted up on the derrick wire and cut into sizeable portions to go into the kettle.

Alex Dan MacKinnon was the cutter on the hartman. Alex was a very strong and seasoned Hebridean whaler. The cuts to the tongue were made at head height, about a foot wide and six feet long. To make the initial cross-cut the cutter had to swing his flensing knife at about shoulder height, then continue with the cut down to the deck. The knife handle and indeed everything else in sight was extremely slippery from the whale oil. Every cutter who handled a knife had to have a piece of sacking round the handle to stop the knife slipping from their grasp.

One day Alex Dan injured his back and was off work. The knife was taken over by another Lewis man, Jimmy MacAulay. Jimmy took a swing with his knife to make his first cut. The knife slipped out of his hand and went flying over my head. It sliced part of the top of the black beret I was wearing, missing my skull by a fraction of an inch. I still break into sweat when I think of it. I cannot remember if I ducked to avoid being decapitated but that was the closest I ever came to death. Everyone had a good laugh and work went on as normal. That was the sense of humour of a whaler.

Working on the hartman was an extremely bloody and dangerous job. There were wires everywhere, all under strain, woven through blocks and tackle in order to place the parts of the whale as close as possible to the kettles. Every hooker was supplied with a steel hook about three feet long. This was a necessary tool to keep oneself stable and from falling over. It was classed as a third hand. By the end of the season I could tie my shoe laces with it. It was a very simple and necessary tool similar to those used by dockers, at least before containerisation.

On a cold icy day working on the hartman was an ideal job if the whale was still fresh – I used to dip my hands in the warm blood. But if the whale was a week old it was certainly not a good job. A week-old whale was held together by the outer blubber. Once the blubber was cut the meat had already turned green and into a liquid soup. There was no chance of putting a wire round the intestines. Instead, all this mess was squeegeed into the kettle. Even with the whale in this horrible state oil was extracted.

In later seasons a product we called 'meat extract' was taken from fresh whale meat. The meat was boiled and liquids pressed out of it, giving an end result that was very similar to Bovril. This particular product was used as a substitute for beef extract in dried soups, and it fetched high prices on the market back home. In the last season I did on the island, 1961, the combined total of meat extract from the two factory ships and the island was 1,300 tons. It was sold on the market at £1,000 per ton.

In 1948 Salvesen fitted out the *Southern Raven* with refrigerators to carry frozen whale meat back to the home market, but it was not a success. Even so soon after the war it was not a popular meat dish to the British. It was eventually sold as pet food. I have to say whale steaks and onions were a favourite dish for me. There is no difference between a good whale steak and a beef steak, as long as it is prepared properly. Chunks of meat about two feet square are cut from the best part of the whale. These are then hung up for a couple of weeks for the oil to drip from it. The outside turns black and pretty hard. This outer layer is then sliced off and the meat inside is beautiful and red, ready to be cut into steaks for the frying pan.

After all the oil and meat extract was separated, the remaining material was put through a drier, bagged and stored for transport to the UK as bonemeal and meat meal, to be used as fertiliser.

Half an hour after the whale was hauled on to the plan-deck, little could be seen of an 80-foot animal.

A blue whale's prick is some size. Air is pumped into the whale when it is killed in order to help it float until it is towed to the factory. When the animal is inflated the penis is pushed out of the body and can be up to three to four feet long. It is so big I have seen whalers making golf bags out of them. I have seen several foetuses inside whales, and the largest I saw, measuring 12 feet, was in an 80-foot blue whale.

The following list shows the approximate dimensions and weights of different parts of a whale:

Measurements

Length	89 feet
Height	10 feet
Circumference	46 feet
Jawbone length	23 feet
Flukes length	18 feet
Fins	9 feet

Weights

Blubber	26 tons (approx.)
Meat	56 tons (approx.)
Bone	22 tons (approx.)
Tongue	3 tons
Lungs	1 ton
Heart	½ ton
Kidneys	½ ton
Stomach	½ ton
Intestines	1½ ton
Liver	1 ton
Blood	8 tons
Jawbone	2 tons
Skull	4½ tons
Backbone	10 tons

Ribs	4 tons
Flukes	1 tons
Fins	1 ton

All the whale-catchers were serviced during the winter months. Each one went to the floating dry dock at Stromness, a neighbouring station which was also owned by Salvesen, to be surveyed and painted. The dry dock had been built in Middlesborough. It was then dismantled and transported to South Georgia where it was re-assembled and used on a regular basis, not only by Salvesen but by other whaling companies including the Russians. Stromness was an old whaling station that had ceased fishing in 1931. It took 20 minutes to sail to it from Leith Harbour. It was there that Shackleton, during his epic expedition to the South Pole, arrived seeking help after his ship, the *Endeavour*, got stranded in the ice. He sailed his lifeboat, the *James Caird*, from Elephant Island where his ship had been stranded, and landed in South Georgia. He then crossed the ice-cap and eventually arrived at Stromness.

The complete fleet of catchers attached to the floating factory ships *Southern Venturer* and *Southern Harvester* and to Leith Harbour must have numbered at least 40. It was some sight to see them all tied up in Jericho Bay. Some catchers were ex-Navy corvettes. They had their bows strengthened and built higher for the harpoon gun. They were faster than the traditionally built whale-catchers and could do up to 17 knots.

The floating factories *Southern Venturer* and *Southern Harvester* arrived at Leith Harbour a few weeks after the fishing season started on their way down to the ice. The catcher men picked up the individual catchers allocated to each factory ship. They were taken alongside the ship, where they loaded up with fuel, harpoons, ropes, wires, shackles, chains and, of course, stores. Leith Harbour was extremely busy over the next few days until the factory ships sailed to their fishing grounds. That was the last time we saw them for at least three months.

When the fishing season ended, the factory ships returned to Leith Harbour, together with their catchers. The catchers were moored in Jericho Bay and everything taken off them. These were ready then to be overhauled by the whalers who had volunteered to overwinter. The volunteers for the winter crew were chosen, and a few days later the factory ships sailed for home.

Considering the weather in the Antarctic, with icebergs, wind, wave and fog, we had very few casualties with our fleet. In 1956 the *Southern Hunter* was lost, but fortunately all her crew were saved. She was fishing with the *Southern Harvester* around the South Shetlands. She was passing through the narrow entrance to Deception and decided to go in and have a look around for whales. As she entered, a large Argentinian ship came steaming out, forcing the *Hunter* to the shore. The propeller hit a rock and the ship was disabled and drifted aground. The crew managed to get ashore but the ship was a total loss.

That was the official account of the loss. In 2009 I met Sir Gerald Elliot, who at one time was a Chairman of Salvesen and is a member of the Salvesen family. He told me he met a crew-member 40 years after the incident who told him the grounding was due to a navigational error by the gunner. The crewman told him there was actually another ship close by but it had nothing to do with the *Hunter* going on the rocks.

4

Overwinter 1961–1962

Two years was a long time without even seeing a woman. When the sea elephants were mating on Stromness Bay one got jealous of them. I was interviewed by the BBC a few years back and was asked, 'Was it hard down in the Antarctic?' I replied, 'Mine was extremely hard when I saw the sea elephants mating, knowing you could not have a woman for another year!'

The winter of 1961–62 proved to be a very long one, because Salvesen decided to close the whaling station in Leith Harbour. This meant the winter was at least six weeks longer than before, as there was no one coming down for the start of a new season for island fishing. The next whalers to arrive would be the *Southern Venturer* and the *Southern Harvester*, returning in six months time.

Everyone settled in for the winter months. The first thing that was done was to remove the compasses from the catchers. The compass contains alcohol, and if left unattended the alcohol was soon drained and swallowed by some hard-drinking whaler.

The men were sorted into gangs. Each gang was allocated a certain job in overhauling all the machinery in the island factory and catchers. There was all sorts of expensive machinery – driers, separators, conveyor belts, cutters, steam-saws, kettles and many, many other bits of plant that I didn't have a clue what they were for. There were workshops for welding, plating, boilermakering, blacksmithing, engineering and radio and asdic operations.

Three gangs were allocated to overhauling the catchers. The deck gang did all the chipping and painting on the decks. The engine-room gang refurbished all machinery in the engine room, and the boilermakers' gang, or the soot gang as they were called, overhauled the two Foster and Wheeler boilers on each catcher. There is little doubt that the soot gang, as the name suggests, had the dirtiest of all jobs and, trust my luck, this was where I was to spend the winter.

My task was to go into the boiler via the furnace hole and inspect the fire bricks, take out any broken ones and call the bricklayer to replace them. Any leaking pipes had to be cut out from the top and bottom by tradesmen. I was still inside the boiler when this work was done. Gas fumes from the oxyacetylene and burning soot were quite overpowering and sometimes actually made me sick. Several times I nearly fainted, but I was determined to carry on. The old tubes were removed and passed through the furnace hole. New ones were installed and welded to the boiler. The tubes were tested by inserting a ball the same bore as the tube. If it travelled freely through the tube then it was OK, but if it stuck that tube had to be renewed. It was not a nice job – there was no protective clothing, no masks and definitely no health and safety.

It was cold down there, bloody cold, and the engineers had a stove they shared with us. The kettle was boiled on it for a cuppa at smoko time. This saved us walking back to the mess room, which was maybe 15 minutes away. From time to time we had some fun at the expense of another gang. We were always thinking up a new prank to play. The most common one played on us was by the deck gang, who would stick a hose down the chimney of the stove just as we were sitting comfortably round it with our coffee. This caused a terrible scene, with ashes, soot, water and fire sparks all over the engine room. Our time for revenge would come when gloves full of soot were scattered all over their newly-painted bulkheads, and so it went on, all in good fun.

We worked 12-hour shifts so the overtime was good, something to look forward to when we were paid off. On Wednesdays we finished at 5 o'clock. This was Kino (cinema) night or time for relaxing. We played a lot of cards, especially cribbage. During one of the competitions I got to the final against another old-time whaler. I was doing well but lost, only to be told later another old whaler was standing behind me telling my opponent what cards I had in my hand. You can't beat an old whaler. Dominos and darts were other popular games. Some of the dart players were capable of playing to a very high standard.

Wednesday was also dobby night, which meant washing our clothes. One of my roommates was the tidiest person I ever met. His clothes were spotless and always ironed. His underpants were always pure white. When he hung them up in the wash-room alongside mine they made me feel quite ashamed. I have to say, though, he did NOT work in the soot gang. One day I decided to soak my Y-fronts in his bucket but under his pants. I did this but unfortunately he got to the bucket before me and I found him wiping his shoes on them. That was the last time I tried that one.

Wednesday night was also a party night. If a brew had been stilled over the previous two weeks, word soon got round that a party was in progress in one or two cabins. This was illegal, of course, and if we were caught everything was confiscated. If the station manager heard through the grapevine that a brew was about to be stilled, he would raid the barracks looking for it. The best place to hide it was in the toilet. The drum would be sat on top of the seat and a pair of boots placed in front of the pan. The door was then locked from the inside and the proprietor of the brew would climb over the top and out of sight. The manager looked underneath the door, saw the boots and left it alone.

It was quite natural for 'cliques' to be formed, especially when it came to stilling. Shetlanders would stick together if they had a brew coming off, and you were really privileged to be invited to join them for a drink. The same applied to the West Coasters. Our language was Gaelic and that was all we spoke to each other. At a party we sang Gaelic songs, so we were also guilty of forming cliques. This particular night four West Coasters had a brew coming off. There was a fifth one, Big Dan, who was aware we were doing this, but he never offered his services by supplying any of the ingredients such as yeast, sugar or fruit. In other words he did not want to take the risk of being caught. He was a big, big man at 6ft 6in but very lazy. As one of us was going down under the foundations to the still he said in Gaelic, 'My knees are bothering me with arthritis, so if you have a drop to spare I would appreciate it.' John, who was on his way down to the still, replied in Gaelic, '*Ged a bhiodh iad a diosgail mar bann-taichean geataichean ifrinn chan fhaigh thu deur foinne!*' 'Supposing they were creaking like the hinges on the gates to hell, you won't get a drop from us!'

During the long winter nights we were entertained by various and accomplished musicians with squeezeboxes, accordions, guitars and mouth organs. As the alcohol mellowed inside them they would start their own party pieces. Some were quite hilarious.

Without doubt we would run out of alcohol during the evening, and all sorts of schemes were thought up as to how one could obtain a bottle from somewhere. This happened one evening at a party I was at. I left the room but didn't tell anyone where I was going. I went down to the office where I got a blank received telegram. I knew Gerry O'Hara, one of the engineers, had a typewriter. Gerry typed out on the telegram: 'A son both well wishing you were home love Mary'. I took the telegram to the Chief Steward, who congratulated me on the birth of my son and gave me a lovely bottle of rum. As I had been in the Antarctic for something like 14 months by this time, Mary must have had the longest pregnancy on record. I went back to the cabin and was the flavour of the night with my mates.

Donald MacKenzie, another seasoned West Coast whaler, told me of a massive Norwegian nicknamed Frankenstein because of his size. Now Frankenstein was a heavy, heavy drinker who had grown a full beard over the winter months. This morning he was terribly dry from the night before. He went down to the Chief Steward and asked for a tot of rum. The steward obliged and actually gave him a large one, which he promptly drank. Frankenstein went back to his cabin, shaved off his beard and went back to the steward for another tot. The Steward didn't recognise him and duly gave him another large tot.

One of my cabin mates during the winter was a very dour and crabbit West Coaster, especially if he had a hangover. One particular evening we had a good party in our cabin. The cabin was cleared up and we turned in. During the morning I was woken up by something pecking on my cheek. I opened my eyes and there staring at me was a poor king penguin. One of the boys had put it in the cabin when we were asleep after the party. The bird had shit all over the cabin floor (there were no carpets). I got up, stepped round the piles of crap and went for breakfast.

When Donald eventually got up he didn't notice the penguin or the mess on the floor. He promptly stepped into everything in his bare feet and went arse over bollocks. We were all waiting for him in the mess room to see what he had to say. It cannot be repeated in this book. Suffice it to say I got the blame.

There were three stations on the island. Grytviken was an Argentine station, a two-hour trip on a catcher from Leith Harbour. The magistrate responsible for law and order for the whole island is based at King Edward Point close to Grytviken. It also has a church built by the Norwegians that has recently been refurbished. Shackleton is buried at King Edward Point, and the cairn on his grave was built by Thomas MacLeod, one of his crew who accompanied both Shackleton and Scott on their expeditions. Thomas MacLeod came from Stornoway, and he is buried in Canada. Husvik was another whaling station in Stromness Bay, about half an hour sailing from Leith Harbour.

During the winter we had one day set aside for sports. Each station took it in turn hosting the winter games. The Norwegians always beat the British at skiing, but we beat them at football. We had races, tug of war, long jump, and high jump. A proper ski jump was constructed. The Norwegians were absolutely experts on skis. They went flying through the air over these jumps. Altogether it was a great day out and a chance to have a chat with whalers from outside our own environment.

There was a piggery on the island with a couple of hundred pigs and a man and young boy to help look after them. One day the men were all sitting in the mess room having their dinner when the chief steward came running in in a panic. He went on to say the pigs, for some unknown reason, were dying. The doctor went over to the piggery and found that several pigs were dead. The ones still alive didn't look too healthy. By evening there were over 100 pigs dumped into the sea. The doctor did a post mortem on a few, and discovered what seemed to be arsenic in their bodies. The swill they were fed with was found to contain arsenic, and an empty tin of arsenic rat poison was found near one of the barracks. By good detective work (not by me) it was established that the young boy who worked with the pig man had purchased a tin of rat poison from the store. He was questioned and admitted administering the poison. Apparently he had fallen out with his supervisor and took his anger out on the pigs. Fresh pork was pretty scarce on the menu after that.

Towards the end of November the *Southern Venturer* and the *Southern Harvester* arrived from home. There was great excitement, as this was the first mail from home for several months. There was gossip in abundance and presents sent down by relatives and friends were exchanged. My present was a bottle of whisky from my mother. That night was quite hectic, with parties in every cabin. There were a few 'dear John' letters, where a girlfriend had decided to give a long-gone whaler the elbow.

The 1961–62 Season

During the next few days Leith Harbour was a very busy place. As mentioned before, fishing from the island was to be discontinued. The whalers who had fished from the island were given jobs on the floating factories. I signed on the *Southern Venturer* on 27 November 1961 for season 61–62. Both factory ships, having supplied the recently overhauled catchers with everything they needed for the coming season, left Leith Harbour to make their way to the fishing grounds in the Weddell Sea and Bellingshausen Sea, a couple of weeks away.

On the way down to the fishing grounds the fleet always fished for sperm whale. The oil and meat from the sperm are not edible and are kept separate. I was amazed when I saw the first sperm whale processed. A third of the body is all head. The head is cut diagonally, and when opened it is completely empty apart from gallons of pure oil. This oil is very expensive and used for fine machinery.

On a rare occasion a sperm whale has a type of growth in its stomach. This is called ambergris. It is carefully cut out and stored separately. I believe it is used in the making of expensive perfume. Unfortunately, during the time I was there, we did not come across any. If my memory serves me right, a whaler from my village was whaling in 1953 or 1954 when his expedition came across a whale with ambergris. It was worth £50 per person. The factory has a crew of 500, so at £50 per person that works out at £25,000 – a valuable growth by any standards.

The machinery in a floating factory is quite amazing – mind-boggling, actually. The amount of plant that takes up several acres ashore in South Georgia is squeezed into a 16,000-ton ship. The whale is hauled on to the deck; the next two decks below are the factory and below them are the tanks. The floating factory processes twice or three times as much as the island, simply because the whale is more plentiful down at the ice. It can process a whale every 20-30 minutes, or an average of 40 per day.

Tankers came down to deliver fuel to the factory ship and take the whale oil back home. Some of these tankers were up to 16,000 tons. The fenders used as buffers between them and the factory ship were two or three whales, and this shows the weight a whale carcase can support.

That season my job was in the stowing gang. The soot gang during the winter was considered cold and dirty, but although the stowing gang was also dirty it was absolutely sweltering, with little or no oxygen. After the meat meal is dried and bagged, it is stored in tanks. The bags, still hot when they are lowered into the tank by wire and winch, arrived one per minute and weighed over a hundredweight each. Each bag was carried on your shoulder and had to be stowed perfectly to avoid it moving during the journey home. The dress you wore was a pair of dungarees cut into shorts, nothing else. The shift was an hour in the tank and an hour off. By the end of your hour on, you ended up breathless, with sweat pouring off you, then it was up on deck where temperatures were below freezing. Not a healthy job.

Homeward-bound during the 1955–56 season, three whalers from the Western Isles lost their lives in Aruba. One went down the tank to recover some empty bags. He got into difficulty so the second man went to his aid. The same happened to him. Then a third went to the rescue, only to suffer the same fate. There was no oxygen left in the tanks. I only mention this terrible disaster to show the reader exactly what it was like in the stowing gang.

There was no time whatsoever for any socialising on the factory ship. It was work, sleep and back to work for three solid months, twelve hours a day, seven days a week. The process of cutting up the whale was exactly the same as on the island. I was a qualified AB when I went whaling and I always wanted to crew a whale-catcher, but it was not to be. Although life on the catcher was hard, there were plenty of volunteers to crew them. Fishing with the floating factory and watching the catchers chasing whales was an eye opener. Norman MacDonald from Stornoway and Gibbie Fraser from Shetland did seven seasons on whale catchers. Norman describes what life was like:

> I went whaling in 1956 and stayed there until the last season, 1963. I spent my life on the whale-catchers. I sailed on the *Southern Wilcox* for four seasons, then two seasons on the *Southern Rover* and one on the *Southern Lily*. The *Southern Lily* was an ex-corvette, much better to work on

than the catchers built for Salvesen. Accommodation was much better – I had a cabin to myself. We had a crew of about 19: a gunner, a mate, an asdic man, radio operator, engineers, four ABs, a cook and two mess boys. When we were 'fast fish' (i.e. with a whale harpooned) everyone turned to. It did not matter whether it was your four hours off, you still had to turn to.

The ABs were paired two to a watch. You did one hour in the barrel (crow's nest) and one hour on the wheel, alternating this for the four hours. I think the most whales my catcher caught in one day was ten. On good days like this you never went to bed. I remember one period when I went 68 hours working without any sleep. We went back to the factory ship every five days, towing a whale to use as a fender. In bad weather or fog the AB was left in charge. The gunner and the mate stayed in their cabins resting.

The wheelhouse was open to the elements, hail, rain or snow. Bad weather and fog was our biggest enemy. The southern ocean can be very eerie in fog, especially when you are surrounded by icebergs. On the other hand a large-sized iceberg can be very useful for shelter in bad weather. It was necessary for everyone to get on with each other on such a small ship.

One day we were fast fish and I was up in the crow's nest. When I came down on deck we heard shouting coming from the hold where the rope is stowed. We went down to have a look and found Duncan MacKay, our radio operator, lying on the deck. His leg, with his boot still on it, was lying beside him. His leg had been caught in the rope that was attached to the harpoon and it had been taken off just below the knee.

We steamed straight away towards the factory ship to get the doctor on board. Doctor Richardson came down in the basket. I was standing on deck with Duncan's leg in my hand. I said to the doctor 'What do you want me to do with this leg?' He replied, 'Throw it overboard – he won't need the leg or the boot again.'

When the fishing season finished I was going home on the *Southern Harvester*. Duncan was still in hospital. I had bought an expensive duty-free watch and I wanted to smuggle it into the UK without paying duty. Duncan took it off me, and when we reached Liverpool he stuck it down between the dressings on his leg, and that's how it arrived in this country.

Norman tells another story of the time they were heading for the start of a new fishing season in South Georgia. They stopped for bunkers (oil) in Caracas, Venezuela. The bumboats as always came alongside to barter their goods 'changy for changy'. Anything of value was sent down to them: trousers, dungarees, jumpers, boots, rope, in fact anything and everything in exchange for booze. The following morning two cabin mates, Roddy MacKenzie and John MacLeod, who had done good business with the bumboats the previous day, woke up with a terrible hangover. John couldn't find his shirt and asked Roddy if he had seen it anywhere. Roddy replied, 'What the hell do you think you were drinking last night?' Roddy's shirt had also gone.

Heading for Home

When our season finished, the *Southern Venturer* and her catchers headed north to South Georgia. Our first job was to lift all the wood covering the plan area and throw it over the side. The ship was then scrubbed clean from top to bottom, including the factory, with caustic soda. This got rid of all the rotten meat and other rubbish that had gathered throughout the season. By the time we reached Leith Harbour the deck at least was fairly clean.

The catchers were tied up in Jericho Bay. Both factory ships always took penguins home to Edinburgh Zoo, but this was to be the last time it would happen. It was a sad time for us whalers too. The *Southern Venturer* was on her last trip, and once we arrived in Liverpool she was sold to the Japanese. It was the last time we saw her. Leith Harbour was closed to British whalers forever, and many of us were in tears. It had been my home for 18 months. We had good times and bad times, but one can only remember the good times. A fully operational factory, with a fully equipped fleet of catchers, was basically left behind and abandoned.

On our way home we were in the Bay of Biscay when news was coming through over the radio that the United States and Russia were preparing for war over the Cuba crisis. I remember thinking, 'I hope we can get home before it starts, and if it does start I will join the Navy.' Thankfully this was not necessary.

Years later, in April 1982, Leith Harbour was headline news for the wrong reasons. Argentina invaded South Georgia on the pretext of collecting scrap metal from Leith Harbour. This was the beginning of the Falklands War. Thankfully we had a Prime Minister, Margaret Thatcher, who stood firm and recaptured the islands. I wrote to Baroness Thatcher and thanked her for saving South Georgia and the Falklands from Argentina and also for saving the country from Arthur Scargill. I sent a bottle of my 'Whaler's Dram' with my letter. Within two days I had a reply from her. Her letter is one of my most treasured possessions and it is framed and hanging in my front room.

After a leisurely trip home I was paid off the *Venturer* on 10 May 1962. She had been my home for the past seven months. We were paid off in the same style as the day we signed on in Leith some 20 months earlier. Local ladies dressed up, their pimps came out in numbers, the bars took on extra staff, as did the police. I cannot say what the priest did, but I doubt if he was overworked. It took a week of celebrations and a few trips to Salvesen's office in Leith for extra subs before I arrived back home in the Western Isles.

5
Home to Lewis

There is little doubt that the arrival of two to three hundred whalers in the islands was good for the local economy. There were weddings every week, an explosion of pregnant women and a baby boom. The local car dealers made a fortune. Every whaler bought a new car, and within a couple of weeks the same car dealers made a fortune repairing them.

These days were before the dreaded breathalyser. I remember one of my best whaling friends from the village was driving home when he was involved in an accident with another car. He was not injured. Within seconds the police were knocking on the driver window and asking him to step out on to the road. He couldn't believe how efficient the local constabulary was and how quick they were on the scene. Yes, you have guessed it: the car he hit was the police car.

The following article was written by my brother Calum, who was 16 when I returned from the whalers:

> Every summer, much like migrating birds, a flock of whalers descended on the island, having spent a season and for some two seasons and a winter, whaling in the South Atlantic.
>
> Never having faced the hazards of that inhospitable environment, it would be wrong of me to comment on the whaler's way of life, but even to an outsider, it is clear that they suffered two privations: lack of female company and no other outlet for their hard-earned cash. Far be it from me to comment on the first one of these, but I played a small walk-on part in the latter.

One of the first things the whalers did when they returned from South Georgia, especially the young ones, was to head for the local car dealers and, as in the gangster films, 'get a set of wheels'. Vauxhall/Bedford was the most popular make at the time, especially the Bedford Dormobile.

In 1962 my brother Jock returned, having overwintered in South Georgia, and like most of his mates he made a beeline for the Vauxhall dealer's garage, emerging with a beautiful Vauxhall Wyvern. To my mind, this car had beautiful lines. It was probably one of the first British cars to have America's GM influence in its styling, with tapering chrome trim along each side of the bonnet. The gear lever was on the steering wheel and it had a single bench seat in the front. The last fact was very useful if the eyelids got heavy, but even more attractive was the fact that the girlfriend could snuggle up close, unimpeded by the gear lever, handbrake and other accoutrements in the front of a modern motor car.

Apart from the bench seat, there was a cavernous glove compartment, but in this case it wasn't used for gloves. It was better than any minibar in the best Hilton Hotel, because it was mobile, always there, and well stocked whenever the notion took you. The previous owner was a Free Church Minister, and if that car could have talked, what stories it could have told about its two owners and their different lifestyles.

True to all or most whalers' traditions, the car was roadworthy for about a month. When one morning at around 6 am he was driving home from a dance, he told me his eyelids got a bit tired and the car ended up in a peat bog. There was enough peat on the chassis to keep the home fires burning for a winter. Once again, true to whalers' tradition, his money ran out after about five weeks and he was off back to the Merchant Navy.

At that time when we came back home from whaling, there was nothing whatsoever to do socially on the island, apart from a dance on a Friday night. The pubs closed at 9 o'clock and there we were with pockets full of money and nowhere to spend it. This led to illegal 'shebeens' sprouting up in villages that were some distance from Stornoway. They were referred to locally as 'bothans'. They were just shacks, some made from the old style thatched cottage, some just sheds erected by local stalwarts, and one I remember was an old bus. We spent many, many enjoyable evenings passing the time of day in them. We also spent a few bob of our whaling money. It was at this stage the operation became illegal, i.e. as soon as money was exchanged for alcohol.

These illegal shebeens were, of course, known to police who tolerated them, but from time to time road traffic accidents happened, some fatal. At such times there would be calls for the police to raid establishments, and the following extract from the *Stornoway Gazette* (who have kindly given me permission to use it) is from one of the resulting court hearings.

> At midnight on 30th March 1967 the 'bothan' at South Dell, Ness was raided by seven police officers led by Sgt Thompson. The building was 19 feet by 11 feet, built of concrete blocks and a felt roof. The small window was covered from the inside with a cardboard box. On entering the officers saw a stove in the centre of the room with seats round all four walls. The building was illuminated by calor gas. In a recess was an 11-gallon beer keg fitted with a tap and a pump. A tray fitted under the beer tap contained pint beer glasses. On this wooden platform there was also a white plastic drip tray. On a seat in the corner was a cash drawer containing £6.0.1. There were also quite a few empty whisky bottles and glasses underneath the seats. Beside the drawer was an empty whisky bottle fitted with a nip measure.
>
> There were seven men present, said Sgt Morrison. 'Do you see any of these men present here?' asked the fiscal.

The Sgt indicated the three men in the dock.

I earlier mentioned that everyone on Lewis had a nickname. The following story features the Vauxhall Wyvern I bought from the minister, and concerns me (Lemon), Butch (Murdo MacKenzie), Stitchy (Alex MacRitchie), Iain Laugy (John MacLeod) and Rashy (Alasdair MacLennan).

Butch takes up the story:

> I was home on leave in 1962 having paid off a Blue Star boat. The whalers came home around the same time. One day you picked me up in the Vauxhall and we went to the next village where we picked up another whaler, Stitchy. Off we went to Stornoway. We were the first in the Mac's Imperial Bar when it opened at five o'clock. There we met another whaler, Ian Laugy, and a local man, Rashy. We stayed there until closing time, nine o'clock in those days. We bought a 'carry out' and off we went to Carloway, some 20 miles away, where Iain Laugy lived. This was the one and only black house I was ever in. I still remember how cosy it was. His mother made us all a meal. After that we went to Ness (30 miles) where we went to the 'bothan'. We had a great time with some of the local whalers we met there. After that we took Iain Laugy home and back to our own village. It was 7.15 am because I remember the workmen waiting for the early morning bus to take them to work. We went to your house where your mother made breakfast. I also remember the tractor was booked to take the peats home. We missed this, which to a crofter is a cardinal sin. I remember going back up town that evening, I can't remember anything else.

This was a typical 48 hours spent by a whaler on his return home. Shortly after that the Vauxhall was a write-off! The 'bothan' was very, very popular.

In 2000 I was interviewed in my pub 'The Whaler's Rest' by Martin Varley. His article was published in the *National Geographic* magazine for October 2000. Mr Varley writes in his last paragraph: 'A century after whalers first began exploiting Antarctic waters, it is they who have become the endangered species.' This is a very true statement. At the age of 70 I am one of the youngest Salvesen whalers alive.

In October 2010 I attended what we believe to be the last Shetland Whalers reunion. There were 250 men from all parts of Scotland. Robin Salvesen, whom I understand is the last to carry the family name, was there. We had a great time. I spoke to one of the whalers and enquired if he knew Jimmy Smith and whether he was still alive. 'Yes,' he said, 'He is very much alive – you are talking to him.' Jimmy had a fantastic memory. He went on to say that the first time we met was when I was on a Blue Star boat in Leith in 1958. I think he was on a Ben boat. 'The next time we met you were on the *Southern Venturer* and I was on a catcher. We came alongside and your mop of ginger hair stuck out like a lighthouse on the deck of the *Venturer*!' Fifty-two years is a long time.

Goodbye to Christian Salvesen, a fine and reputable company who looked after their whalers. And goodbye, old friends, I am proud to have gone whaling with you.

My last trip in the Merchant Navy was on the MV *Ireland* to Italy – Salerno, Palermo, and Naples, typical Mafia land. (Little did I know then that my next career would be in the police.) I signed on on 6 September 1962 and was paid off on 24 October 1962. My gross wage for that trip was £120.1.9 (one hundred and twenty pounds, one shilling and nine pence). After deductions my payslip showed a balance due of £1.00. This just demonstrates what a great time was had by all!

I remember when we were on the way home and going through the Straits of Gibraltar, my cabin mate, who was in the top bunk, woke up. His legs were dangling over the side of the bed. I wondered why he was not getting up and asked what was wrong. He replied, 'Jock, have a look at this.' I got up and there he was with his penis in his hand. It was dripping a bit. The Italian lady he was with in Naples had obviously given him a present he did not want – a dose of VD. He was a Cockney AB, and although I cannot remember his name or his face, I can certainly remember his prick.

6

Joining the Met

I stayed ashore in London for a few weeks working as a rigger with Blue Star Line. The winter of 1962–63 was the last of the 'London Smog' winters. These were quite frightening, actually, especially when you were walking down to the docks at four in the morning to see off a ship. The fog was so thick the conductress walked in front of the bus for the driver to follow. It was eerie when you did not know what you might bump into next. Also, the streets around the docks were not the safest to be walking in this type of weather.

It was the coldest winter ever, just like being back in the Antarctic. I remember sitting in a bosun's chair and heaving myself up the mast to squeegee it down, and a bucket of boiling water left on the deck and ready to be pulled up after me was frozen by the time it got to the top of the mast. I found that winter more severe than any I did in the Southern Oceans.

Every Saturday evening we met up with friends from home at the Lewis Club in Fetter Lane in the City. This was a thriving club formed before the First World War. In 1963 two of our club members got married, and it was at their wedding I met my dear wife Donalda.

The old Lewis Club folded due to lack of support. In 1964 a few of the members met in a pub in Paddington, and that night we founded 'The Highlands and Islands Society of London'. I am proud to have been a founder of a society which is still going strong. Most members in those days spoke Gaelic. Scottish dance music and songs were in full swing and enjoyed by everyone. Sailors and members of the armed forces stationed in

London and the Home Counties met there every Saturday. It was home from home.

Our regular watering hole was the Clachan Bar in Fleet Street, which was next door to the Scottish Corporation dancehall. The latest gossip from home was discussed and copies of the *Stornoway Gazette* were exchanged. Needless to say, we also had a good skinful!

I had been toying with the idea of joining the Metropolitan Police, but had never taken it any farther. Then one Saturday night I was on the No 15 bus returning to my digs in Plaistow. The bus stopped outside a Police Station in Commercial Road. On the spur of the moment I got off the bus and staggered into the front office. I could see the look on the sergeant's face – 'No, not another drunk!' Anyway, I asked for the forms to join up. He laughed his head off. 'Are you serious?' he said. I told him I had never been more serious in my life.

It was around October 1962 when I posted off the application forms, and I sat the entrance exam for the Met on New Year's Day 1963 – not a very suitable day for a Scottish whaler. There was an all-night party up in King's Cross, and as usual I was the last to leave. It was snowing heavily and I had to get a taxi from King's Cross to Plaistow where I was staying. I put on a fresh change of clothing and then took the underground to Borough High Street where I was to sit the exam.

I was confident I would pass the medical, but dubious as to whether I would pass the written part of the exam. The knowledge and reasoning was pretty straightforward. The final part was an essay. When I turned the paper over there was a choice of three subjects. I couldn't believe my eyes when I saw that one of the choices was 'A trip down whaling'. I was pretty sure now I would pass.

I still have a copy of the Metropolitan Police brochure for recruits. The pay for a constable was £600.00 per annum, increasing to £700.00 after two years plus £20.00 a year London allowance.

Training to be a Police Officer

On 8 April 1963 I started my training at Peel House, Regency Street, in London, an old Victorian building just north of Vauxhall Bridge. My weekly wage was £12 3s. 5d. Training lasted for 13 weeks, and I was very proud when I was fitted out with my new uniform. Discipline was hard to swallow after having spent the previous two years in the wild Antarctic. Parades and marching were not something I was accustomed to. I failed miserably with my marching, and to this day I have not mastered this simple art. I can never keep in step with the person in front of me. This was very embarrassing when on parade. There was another student in my class who had the same problem, and the two of us were the laughing stock of the recruits as we were marched up and down the parade ground on our own.

Halfway through the course we were called out to assist with crowd control when Princess Alexandra and Angus Ogilvy got married. This was the first time training school officers had been used since the coronation of King George VI. We were on duty outside Buckingham Palace and closely supervised by a sergeant. It was certainly a far cry from a croft in the Outer Hebrides and from my days in South Georgia.

At Peel House the classrooms were downstairs and we stayed in dormitories above them. There was no privacy whatsoever. If someone farted there were shouts of 'dirty bastard!' or you were showered with fruit (rotten if possible), soap bars or anything moveable. If you snored, a bucket of water was thrown over the partition.

I remember the night Henry Cooper was fighting Cassius Clay, as he was then called. Geoff Watts and I were wrestling up on the top floor. The house sergeant, Sergeant Scott, caught us and gave us a bollocking. On top of that he sentenced us to a week washing dishes in the canteen. I found this hard to swallow and petty. I felt extremely frustrated and angry. After all I was 22 years of age, had sailed round the world several times, and had spent two years in the Antarctic – perhaps something Sergeant Scott had never done.

During weekends students who were able to return by 8 am on Monday were allowed home. The Scots, Irish and Welsh students were the only ones left around. Halfway through the course the Highland Games were held on Clapham Common. I was looking forward to this weekend, and as I had been such a good boy for the previous six weeks I decided it was about time I let my hair down. This was always a big day for the London Scots, and was usually attended by every Gaelic-speaking sailor who happened to be in port. There were plenty of Gaelic singing competitions, ceilidhs, pipe music, accordion music and of course a beer tent. As expected I met friends in the tent who found it hard to believe I had joined the police.

While we were attending Training School we had to be indoors by 11 pm. The 'boot room' was in the basement, and we always left the window open so that if we came in late we could climb in unnoticed. The night of the Highland Games I arrived at Peel House around 2 am, pretty much under the weather. Instead of going in via the boot-room window as I should have done I went to the main entrance. The warden came to the door and refused me entry. He told me it was after 11 pm and I was not allowed in. I told him I didn't ask for the time, barged past him and made my way upstairs to my room.

I was just about to get into bed when there was a knock on the door. There was my favourite Sergeant Scott. He cautioned me and told me he was reporting me for being drunk. I told him where to go. All the other students in the dormitory could hear this conversation and they were pissing themselves. 'You're in the shit tomorrow, Jock!' they sang.

Jock Dodds was the Commandant of the training school, a good man who treated us as men. After parade on Monday morning, Sergeant Scott marched me – or tried to march me – up to Mr Dodd's office. I had my helmet under my arm and saluted in a way I thought would impress the Commandant. Instead I got a bollocking, as you are not supposed to salute unless you are wearing your helmet. Not a good start to proceedings.

Sergeant Scott gave his evidence as follows:

> On Sunday 6th May at 2.05 am in room 15 of the section house I saw PC Murray. He was undressed and about to go to bed. His speech was slurred, his eyes were glazed. He was drunk, sir. I introduced myself, told him I was reporting him for being drunk and cautioned him and he said 'Off you go, I am going to bed.' I must say, sir, he was a polite drunk.

The Commandant said to me, 'Is that correct, PC Murray?'

'I can't remember, sir,' was my answer.

His response was to ask, 'Do you want to go back fishing to Stornoway?'

'I would prefer to go back whaling to the Antarctic, sir, where I have just come from,' I said.

He looked at my favourite Sergeant with a slight grin on his face, scratched his head and sentenced me to two weeks in the canteen washing dishes, on top of the week I was already doing. I had fully expected the sack, but Jock Dodds was a man's man who had served in the war.

My First Posting

I survived training school and was posted to Gerald Road B Division, covering the Chelsea area of London. Gerald Road is in the heart of Knightsbridge and Belgravia. My wage was then increased to £13 9s 10d. I had a few wage increases afterwards as follows: on 1 December 1964 it was increased to £15 6s 8d. On 8 April 1965 we had a further rise to £15 18s 2d. On 1 January 1966 there was another rise to £16 17s 4d, followed by a further increase to £18 6s 1d on 1 March 1967. On 8 April 1967 I achieved £18 19s 6d, and my last increase shown in pounds, shillings and pence was on 8 April 1968: £19 12s 11d.

Gerald Road was my working station for the next seven years. I would say this was the happiest and most carefree time of my police career, and I am still in contact with colleagues who served with me there. The building is no longer a police station but is now a private dwelling. Its function has been replaced by Belgravia Police Station.

When I joined, most of the serving officers were ex-servicemen who had served in the war. Many were coming to the end of their careers as police officers. They had seen and done it all, and were, as far as I am concerned, good tutors. Nothing flustered them and they stood for no bullshit from anyone. I was still learning beats when I was paired off with an old PC. If my memory serves me right his name was MacAdam. We were walking down Buckingham Palace Road, and as we got to the junction of Lower Belgrave Street a car parked right in front of us, blocking our way, which meant we would have to walk round the car. The driver got out and was about to lock the door. MacAdam climbed onto the bonnet, walked across it and down the other side. He didn't bat an eyelid and carried on. When I joined him I said 'You can't do that!' He replied, 'I've just done it – he won't park like that again.' The owner of the car never said a word, but I noticed he took the hint and moved it.

When Gerald Road closed for good several years after I left, all officers who served there were invited to a street party. The surrounding streets were closed off and tables were placed in the middle of Elizabeth Street laden with food and drink. Local residents and Members of Parliament who lived on our patch (and there were many) were invited. It was a great reunion and a resounding goodbye to a fantastic little station.

I was staying in a Police Section House in Beak Street, right in the middle of Soho, and life was perfect. One unfortunate incident springs to mind, however, which, to be honest, upset me. On 11 July 1963, a matter of weeks after I joined the police, King Paul and Queen Frederika of Greece were on a visit to London. A well-documented incident occurred which has been called 'The Brick Case'.

The royal visitors were staying in Claridge's Hotel. Police were anticipating trouble with demonstrators and all leave was cancelled. The previous night a Police Inspector was hit in the face with a brick, inflicting a wound that needed nine stitches.

Harry 'Tanky' Challenor was a respected Detective Sergeant attached to West End Central Police Station. He had served in the SAS during the war in Sicily, Italy and France, and was well known in the West End by hardened criminals, pimps, prostitutes, porn-shop owners, club-owners and thieves alike. I had never met Tanky at that stage, but I had heard stories of him because I was staying in the same section house as one of the 'Aides to CID' who worked with him.

On the night of the demonstration Harry was in charge of three junior detectives. They arrested a demonstrator and found a brick on him. It was alleged they planted this brick and all four officers were arrested. They subsequently appeared at the Old Bailey where they were convicted. Challenor was found 'unfit to plead'. Two of the other officers, both aged 26, were sentenced to four years' imprisonment and the youngest, aged 21, was sentenced to three years. He was the one in the section house with me. He was a nice boy who at that young age lost his job and all prospects for the future. Harry was a formidable character who worked extremely hard for the Commissioner. It was a sad ending for him and the young lads who were with him. A few years later I was living very close to Harry Challenor in Sutton, Surrey. He wrote a book afterwards called *Tanky Challenor* that is well worth reading.

Gerald Road had everything. The television series *Upstairs Downstairs* was filmed in Eaton Square next door to our station. We covered from the Albert Hall to Sloane Square, King's Road, Embankment and back up to Victoria Station, up to Hyde Park Corner and then down Knightsbridge. We had a mixture of everything. King's Road in the swinging 60s was an eye-opener. We had the Beatles living in William Mews and a PC was posted outside their house day and night to keep fans at bay. Every evening and weekend thousands of fans turned up and had to be controlled by officers from Gerald Road. The Rolling Stones lived in Chelsea, if my memory serves me right, in Cheyne Walk. There was never a dull moment for a young PC who fancied a bit of skirt – hot pants and miniskirts were the fashions of the day. This was an excellent breeding ground (I don't mean sex-wise!) for a young copper. The Chelsea Flower show was another great attraction.

We covered Victoria Station and Victoria Bus Station. We had Chelsea and Knightsbridge barracks, the Royal Albert Hall and the KLM, BOAC and British Caledonian air terminals, so there was no shortage of passing trade. The top half of our patch consisted of Belgravia, Knightsbridge, and Eaton Square and was the richest area of London. In contrast, Pimlico by the Thames was made up of council estates, and one of them, Churchill Gardens, was the largest estate at that time in Europe. It had a good variety of people and crime.

We had numerous embassies on our ground – Turkish, Hungarian, Iranian, Irish, Spanish and many others – and if there was any political unrest in their countries we had to have a PC assigned to them as a fixed post. I was posted to the Spanish Embassy one night when I saw a man interfering with cars on the inside of the square. I watched him closely as he tried the door-handles of several cars.

At that time the 'Sus' (suspicion) law was our bread and butter. I had enough evidence to arrest him on suspicion of loitering with intent. As I went to arrest him he was off and over the fence surrounding the square. This fence was six feet high. I made the bold effort of jumping the fence after him, but my heavy overcoat caught on the fence and I was left hanging like Norman Wisdom usually ended up in his films. I had cut my hand and it made the local newspaper. When I told the inspector what happened he gave me a bollocking for leaving my fixed post. 'Crazy!' I thought, 'what a thank you for trying to do your job!'

By far the most frightening duty I experienced was working the old-style 'plug and cord' telephone switchboard. I didn't have a clue where to start. There were cords and plugs everywhere, with extension holes flashing with calls from an angry impatient senior officer. Every time I was on the switchboard you could take it for granted a senior officer would pop his head round the corner to see who the useless operator was, and as they left I could hear them muttering, 'I knew it would be Jock.' However, it had one advantage. Our telephonist was Penny, a lovely lady who had the most beautiful pair of boobs. She wore low-cut dresses, very low for that period. Probationers like me stood behind her whilst she gave us instructions on how to cope with the switchboard. This gave us an excellent opportunity to view her very deep cleavage, the valley of our dreams.

During the 1960s this country was still under the threat of a nuclear attack. The government of the day took this seriously and contingency plans were set out, some of which involved the police. We were given war manuals and instructions on what to do should an attack take place. We had to attend instruction classes, where we were told what life would be like in the event of an air attack and what it would involve in the days and weeks afterwards. Radiation and the effect it has on people were explained to us. We were shown instruments used to measure the amount of radiation in the air.

With the possibility of a two-day early warning system, it was anticipated that both the Metropolitan Police and the City of London Police would be responsible for organising the evacuation of people from the City to the countryside. This would be done using a 'Mobile Column'. The Mobile Column was made up of several coaches and lorries equipped with mobile kitchens, various machines and stores suitable for such an operation, together with motor-cycle outriders. Fifty to sixty officers were attached. They were to be self-sufficient in all aspects. Once the column reached a destination nominated by senior officials and at a place free from radiation, camp would be set up.

The Mobile Column went off on a two-week training exercise. Each officer had a specific job, for example some were cooks, some drivers and some radio operators. Field Hygiene Officers were responsible for all water and sanitary needs.

When this exercise was under way, police forces throughout England were informed, and should a major incident occur the Mobile Column could be called in to assist. This might be in the event of a plane or rail crash, or to search large areas of open ground in the case of a murder or a lost person.

Luckily we did not have a nuclear war, and the Mobile Column is a thing of the past. It was a very enjoyable two weeks, though, and I would compare it to what the Territorial Army does nowadays. When one looks back I still think the whole operation was farcical. We would never have managed to evacuate eight million people using these methods. I believe now, as I did then, that these arrangements were utterly useless.

If the older PCs thought a probationer was a little timid, they soon took advantage of this. For example, we as constables had to cover school crossings, which we all hated. It was during the early 60s that school crossing lollipop men and ladies were introduced. When the lollipop stick first came out, one of the old sergeants gave this young PC one and had him patrolling Pimlico Road, testing it for wind resistance. The poor boy spent all morning marching up and down the street until he was due to come in for refreshments.

On another occasion there was a circus coming to Clapham Common. In order to give it publicity the owners decided to cross Chelsea Bridge with some of the animals, one of which was a huge elephant. They were walking up Lupus Street when the poor elephant stepped on a round coal-hole lid and one of its feet went straight through it. This incident happened on the beat of the above-mentioned PC. He did not witness the incident but was soon told by a member of the public who had seen what happened. The PC made his way down to the scene.

We had no radios in those days but we did have a police box

at the end of Lupus Street. The PC made his way to the box to inform the station of what he had come across and to seek advice. The telephonist passed him on to the station officer who immediately gave him a bollocking for taking the mickey and wasting police time. The station officer didn't believe him until an excited member of the public called in to the station. Back-up officers were sent to Lupus Street and the animal was eventually freed by a keeper who entered the coal cellar and managed to push the elephant's foot back up.

For the first two years after leaving training school, the probationer had to attend instruction classes once a fortnight or once a month, I cannot remember which. Some of us who were workers hated this, but others who eventually ended up as our senior officers quite enjoyed it. I considered myself a worker, and if possible I made sure I had an arrest or was attending court on the day classes were held.

I just could not study, and when in class I would go out of my way to distract the instructor. Inspector Clark, who was an instructor, was a gentleman. He hated anyone chewing gum or sweets in class. My friend John Batey was a good worker, an excellent thief-taker. He also tried to avoid classes as much as possible. This particular day John had a bag of toffee sweets, quite hard to chew. I noticed he was chewing a gob-full. He must have had three or four in his mouth at once. I asked him for a sweet and he willingly gave me the bag to pass it round the class. When I was satisfied everyone had a sweet I stuck up my hand and said, 'Please sir, John Batey is eating sweets.' John had too many sweets in his mouth and was unable to swallow quickly enough before Inspector Clark arrived at his desk.

'PC Batey,' he enquired, 'are you chewing?'

John struggled to say, 'Noooo, noooo, sir,' and he nearly choked. Clark made John get up and spit the mouthful out in the bin in front of the class. When John was able to speak again he pointed at me and shouted, 'I've given that bastard a bagful!' The rest of the class just carried on chewing. Great days!

7

Working in A Division

In 1965 the Greater London Council changed its boundaries. Gerald Road then changed to A Division. This meant we covered Buckingham Palace and all royal palaces throughout the country, the Palace of Westminster, Hyde Park and numerous embassies. It was boring for a keen officer to be standing on a fixed post for four hours. The best embassy posting of all was the Hungarian Embassy. George Blake had been arrested for spying and held in Brixton Prison. He escaped from prison and was supposedly taken to the Hungarian Embassy and from there to an Eastern Bloc country. This was the reason we had a fixed post there.

The porter was a really friendly character, and I suspect an alcoholic, who may or may not have been trying to cultivate us young PCs to gain information. As far as I was concerned it was the complete opposite. I tried to cultivate him as an informant, but without much success. Every morning at 6 am when we changed shifts he was at the door with a bottle of apricot brandy. I don't think many of my colleagues accepted his offer, but I never refused to join him in the porch for a few glasses. I am still none the wiser if Blake actually escaped via this embassy or not. No one was ever arrested for assisting him.

During the morning and evening rush hour, most major junctions were controlled by PCs. Victoria Street had five roads merging outside Victoria Station. Control of the junction was shared between Rochester Row Police Station and Gerald Road Police Station. For one particular three-week period I shared this junction with Iain Morrison, a fellow islander who was stationed at Rochester Row. Iain was brought up in London but spoke fluent Gaelic. We decided that for the next three weeks we would only speak Gaelic to each other and pretend we did not have any English. Anyone who approached us for directions was answered in Gaelic, and anyone asking for any sort of information or assistance was answered in Gaelic. Tourists thought we were mad, but we kept this up for most of the three weeks, until one day we noticed a lady approaching us together with an Inspector. We had a good idea what was coming, so when the lady repeated her complaint to the Inspector in front of us we reverted back to English. The lady was gobsmacked, and that was the end of the complaint. When Iain left the Met he emigrated to Canada. He was killed in a mining accident there, but his remains were taken back to the Isle of Lewis to be buried in his beloved village of Uig.

Traffic duty was a horrible job, especially on a wet and windy day. Fumes from the cars were nauseating, and by the end of your tour you coughed up black phlegm. To pass the time some of us used to chat up the 'dolly birds', and many a PC found a wife on a traffic posting. There was one PC who, when on traffic duty at Chelsea Bridge, used to line up all the motorcycles by the stop line. He had a white handkerchief tied to his truncheon. When it was time to let that line of traffic go he raised his truncheon above his head then lowered it and shouted 'Go!' There would be a scramble of motorcycles to see who would get pole position. The early morning commuters loved him. Can one imagine a PC doing that today? Even if he did, what would the consequences be?

I was still at Gerald Road in 1969 when the IRA started their campaign of violence in Northern Ireland. The Commissioner of the day wanted trained negotiators who could speak Gaelic and were to be readily available should a siege situation or a plane hijacking occur involving the IRA.

Along with Duncan Macrae, a Gaelic-speaking PC from Applecross who was stationed at West End Central, I was selected for training on this course. Our Gaelic is similar to Irish Gaelic. We were taken to London Airport with an Assistant Commissioner. A plane was set aside for the training purposes, complete with passengers. Duncan boarded the plane and was acting the part of the spokesman for 'the IRA men' who had just hijacked the plane. Then the fun began – no one knew what we were saying. The Assistant Commissioner would tell me what to say to Duncan, who would then give a completely hilarious answer. We went on taking the piss for a while, until the Assistant Commissioner heard one of us saying the word 'overtime'. He knew he had not mentioned anything to us involving that word. I think I was saying to Duncan in Gaelic, 'Tell him not to cut down on our overtime' (neither of us knew the Gaelic for overtime). It was then the Assistant Commissioner twigged that we were messing about.

Duncan is the only officer I know who served on the Flying Squad at every rank from DC to Superintendent. He now drives a London taxi and is as happy as Larry.

My First Arrest

My first arrest was man named Ernie Atha, a down-and-out aged around 60, homeless, with no relatives to my knowledge. He tried to earn a few bob as what we called a luggage tout. In the early 60s there was no transport other than taxis between Victoria Railway Station and Victoria Coach Station. Homeless people like Ernie (and there were a few of them) who saw anyone struggling with a suitcase asked if they could assist them, and in return got a tip. This was quite a good service to passengers in some ways, but as suitcases used to go missing it became our duty to put a stop to it.

The law said we had to give two verbal warnings before we could arrest luggage touts for footway obstruction. On my second day on the streets patrolling on my own, I saw our bold Ernie approaching a lady who was carrying a suitcase. I spoke to Ernie with intention of giving him a verbal warning, and he just took off in the direction of the police station. I was pretty close behind telling him I had not arrested him. Ernie was muttering, 'Yes, you have', while I was saying, 'No, I haven't.' 'Yes, you have.' 'No, I haven't.' This conversation went on all the way to the police station.

By this time I was panicking, but Ernie would not listen. He opened the door, walked in and gave all the evidence about the offence to Sergeant Marcantonio, who was the desk sergeant. I told the sergeant I had not arrested Ernie but had given him a verbal warning. By this time I was feeling pretty sheepish and embarrassed. Sergeant Marcantonio said, 'Ernie himself has given me the best evidence of arrest I have ever heard, so you have arrested him – OK, PC Murray?' Ernie had been arrested so often for the same offence that he knew the evidence required off by heart. He just wanted a bed for the night. Our older PCs gave me a lot of ribbing over this.

Courtship and Marriage

I met my wife Donalda at the wedding of a friend. Donalda was a nurse training in the Royal Free Hospital, which in those days was in Gray's Inn Road, and she was sitting opposite me at the table during the reception. I had never met her or even seen her before but for me it was love at first sight. We were married within the year, and she has been my rock ever since.

Throughout the year we were courting I was on my best behaviour, at least when she was present. I was determined not to lose her, so much so I used to attend church with her, something I didn't look forward to. As always I ended up putting my foot in it. Donalda came from a practising Christian family. Her mother's identical twin, auntie Kennag, was also a practising Christian and attended the same church. One lived in Kentish Town and the other in Camden Town, not too far away from each other. At that time I did not know London very well. I was one of the few attending the church that possessed a car, an A40 Somerset.

The first day I met her in church I was introduced to her mother and father and also auntie Kennag. After the service finished there was the usual chitchat outside. It was then my time to show off with my car. Donalda was talking to one of the twins who I thought was her mother. I offered them both a lift home, which was accepted. I was heading for Kentish Town where I knew Donalda lived, but she directed me to Camden Town where her auntie lived. It was then I realised I had taken her auntie home and left her parents at the church to make their way home by bus and train. Not a good start for a love-struck copper. It took me a long time to live that one down.

I had my stag night in December 1964 in the Clachan Pub in Fleet Street. A few seamen whom I had sailed with were there, and a good night was had by all. Afterwards I gave the sailors a lift down to the docks in my car. My uniform was on the back seat. As I dropped them off by the dock gates, one of them, a wind-up merchant, started shouting, 'Police, help! Police, help!' On hearing the shouting, the Port of London Authority Police came running over. I put the car in gear and made good my escape. There is a strong possibility that I was over the limit, although there was no breathalyser in those days. I cursed that bloody seaman, as I could have lost my job before I really had started it.

The following morning I was on early turn. I drove to the station to get changed and found that one of my boots was missing. One of the sailors had nicked it. I had to parade with one boot and one shoe, and for the next eight hours I was walking with a severe limp. That was the last bunch of seamen I ever gave a lift to.

On the first night that I was away from home after we got married I lost my wedding ring. Three of us had travelled to Holyhead to escort some prisoners back to London. It meant an overnight stay and we joined the local officers for a drink, ending up in a nightclub. The following morning I noticed my wedding ring had gone, and I still don't know how I lost it. My wife never noticed and after a week I had to tell her. I said I thought I might have left it in the train toilet. She believed me, and to this day we have never questioned our faith in each other.

Early Experiences on the Beat

For the first two weeks at a station a probationer PC is paired with an experienced constable. When on night duty and early turn, the first and last thing the officer does is to check all shops and business premises to make sure they are secure. We had a crude but, when one thinks of it, an ingenious way of marking the premises we had checked earlier. We just jammed a match in the door recess. We would know the door had been interfered with if the match had dropped to the ground. A more thorough inspection would then be carried out. This particular morning I was paired off with Peter Bateman, who became a lifelong friend. We crossed over Elizabeth Bridge, and when we got to the junction of Hugh Street, Peter told me to check all the shops to the right and he would check all the shops to the left. After this we were to meet up in Eccleston Square.

I finished checking my side and made my way to our meeting point. Whilst I was waiting for Peter I noticed someone sleeping on a bench by the church. I went over and tried to wake the person up. He was obviously a vagrant. When Peter arrived I told him I couldn't wake the person. Peter took one look at him and said, 'No wonder – he's dead.' We searched him and found papers to show he had been bailed from Gerald Road only some two hours beforehand. I wondered if he was bailed out dead!

In 1966 there was a seamen's strike. This was only two years after I had finished with the sea myself, so I knew most of the sailors. The strike went on for quite some time. They had several marches in central London, and I was part of the police contingent marching with them. John Prescott had by this time climbed up the ladder and was a Seamen's Union delegate. After a couple of weeks the boys were running short of dough. I lent some of them the odd fiver until they were in a position to repay me.

In 2009 I was approached in our local post office on the Isle of Lewis by a retired seaman. He took out his wallet and handed me a carefully folded £5 note. I asked him what it was for, as I had not seen him for some 50 years. He said, 'Remember the seamen's strike back in 1966? Well, I borrowed £5 from you then and it gives me great pleasure to pay it back. I didn't want to go to your pub to give it to you, as I knew I would leave there pissed.' I told him to give it to his grandchildren.

The Great Train Robbery took place in 1963, shortly after I joined. The details of several vehicles used by the robbers were circulated to all forces in an attempt to trace them. Tony Mitchell, a new officer who joined the Met after doing his National Service in the RAF, was someone who never forgot a vehicle registration number. One day we were walking up towards Knightsbridge, and when we got to Lowndes Square, he stopped, pointed out a Ford Cortina and said, 'Jock, that's one of the vehicles used in the train robbery.' The number began JJJ – I cannot remember the rest – and sure enough he was right. The car was seized.

Churchill's Funeral

Sir Winston Churchill was buried on 30 January 1965. I well remember this for three reasons. Firstly, it was one of the coldest days I can recall in all the time I served as a police officer. It was made colder by the fact one was standing still for hours, lining the route of the funeral procession. The second reason was because I was late for duty, and thirdly, I was starving. Nowadays when officers are engaged on policing demonstrations and the like, they have a catering kitchen which supplies a three-course meal. In the 60s we were given a pork pie, nothing else. It was a long, long day.

We were all dressed in No. 1 uniform, which was only worn on ceremonial occasions. The three-quarter length jacket was buttoned up to the neck, and worn with a black leather belt and white gloves.

One hundred officers from Gerald Road had to parade in Elizabeth Street at 6 am. We were to march down to Parliament Square and become part of the line on the route for crowd control. I was staying at that time in a police flat very close to the station. Having previously served as a seaman doing watch duties, I never had any problems getting up in the morning. On this very important day I was late for the first and last time of my service.

The officers involved in the parade had already moved off and were about to cross Ebury Street when I joined up with them. I have already mentioned my problems marching properly, so it must have been quite hilarious for anyone watching me trying desperately to fall into step. Having somehow managed this I was gaining confidence, when the order 'parade halt' came. Everyone bumped into each other like a pack of dominos. This was a bogus order, given by a PC who was at the rear of the parade and marching beside me.

Sergeant John Friend (he was not friendly) was leading the parade that morning, and he was jumping up and down like a lunatic trying to find out who gave the order. I believe he blamed me as I was the latecomer. Eventually we brushed ourselves down, straightened our helmets and off we went again. Our Sergeant never found out who the culprit was. Candid Camera would have had a field day!

During the mid-1960s a lot of changes took place within the Met. In 1965 the boundaries of the divisions were reorganised and some stations changed from one division to another. Gerald Road Police Station changed from 'B' to 'A' division. The black badges on our helmets were changed to silver. When I joined we wore blue shirts with a collar and stud, but we were changed to white shirts. I liked the previous shirt with the detached collar which was starched and looked smart.

Our No.1 uniform was done away with and so was the greatcoat. We were issued with a lighter uniform which was an improvement on the old serge. Our very adaptable capes were also discontinued.

When I joined all our vehicles were black. The 'Black Maria' overnight became a 'White Maria', and the black Wolsley 690 area car became a white Rover 2000. Then the panda car arrived in different colours, and the 'noddy bike' (police motorcycle) in grey. We as PCs complained that the change of colour made it a lot easier for villains to spot us at night, but this fell on deaf ears. We soon got used to it.

Officers from 'A', 'B' and 'F' divisions covered Chelsea, Fulham and Queens Park Rangers football matches. The Chelsea manager at the time was Tommy Docherty. He had an excellent young team who were a joy to watch, including Charlie Cooke, Eddie McCreadie, Peter Osgood, Chopper Harris, Ian Hutchinson and many others.

I was on duty at Chelsea's home ground, Stamford Bridge, one day and was posted to the stands in the Shed. As usual there was shouting and swearing at the opposition. My ear tuned in to a group of four who were definitely not English. On moving closer I realised they were a group of islanders shouting and swearing in Gaelic. No one could understand what they were saying apart from me. When I went over to them and told them in Gaelic, '*Tha sibh deanamh fuam ifrinneach*' (You are making a hell of a noise), they couldn't believe their ears. I joined them for a drink after the game.

Tommy Trinder was the Chairman of Fulham, whose home ground was Craven Cottage. They had an equally talented team, with Bobby Robson, Johnny Haynes, George Cohen and Jimmy Hill. I always enjoyed Craven Cottage. It was a little compact ground and spectators were close to the pitch. Chelsea charged us 2p for a cup of tea, while Fulham gave us tea for nothing. I have supported Fulham ever since.

It was during this period that the Kray Brothers were at their most active, but I was not really involved with them. They owned a club, Esmeralda's Barn, in Wilton Street, Knightsbridge. The place was obviously under surveillance by Squad officers who were at the time targeting them, and I was one of the uniformed officers given the job of noting the car registrations of their customers. Later, when I was on the drug squad, Charlie Kray, the older one of the brothers, was one of our targets. I spent many hours following him and he was eventually convicted.

8
CID Years

I spent four happy years in uniform, but eventually I felt I was getting a bit stale and not performing to the best of my ability. I thought a change would give me a kick up the arse, but at the same time I felt I didn't have the confidence to be a CID officer. My name was always on the good 'arrest sheet' for crime offences. This sheet of paper was posted on a weekly basis in the canteen. This brought me to the notice of Fred Lambert, who was the Detective Inspector. He called me into his office and suggested I apply to join the CID. I have a copy of my original application. It is endorsed by Ken Newman, our superintendent at the time. Years later, Sir Kenneth, as he became, was the Commissioner when I was presented with my long service and good conduct medal at Hendon. He had a smile on his face when he said, 'I'm pleased you made it, Jock.'

I have suffered from a hearing problem since childhood. My mother always thought I was purposely ignoring her. In fact in the end I was medically discharged from the police and had to retire with only 27 years' service because of my hearing. When you apply to join the CID you have to go on a selection board at Scotland Yard. This takes place in a large room in front of a Commander and two Chief Superintendents who are sitting a fair way from where the applicant is sitting. At my first selection board the Commander asked me, 'PC Murray, do you read *Police Gazettes*?' My answer was, 'No, sir, I was never in the Police Cadets.' Needless to say, I failed that time.

When first transferred to the CID you were given the title 'Aide to CID'. You spent all the time patrolling in plain clothes, following suspects, arresting suspects and assisting CID officers with major enquiries. From time to time one got posted to the Q car. This was considered a quality posting, and indeed it was. We were given roving commission to take calls over the radio and go anywhere. In 1966 three officers from 'F' division were shot and killed in Shepherds Bush while they were patrolling in the Q car. They had stopped three suspects who were driving a Standard Vanguard car. The driver, Harry Roberts, calmly got out and shot the three officers. Firearm offences were on the increase in the 1960s.

One time I was posted to a six-week tour on the Q car. I cannot recall who my driver was. One evening, around 8 o'clock, we had a call: 'Suspects on the roof of a building in Morpeth Street at the rear of Westminster Cathedral.' On arrival we were met by a nun in full habit, who informed us the premises were part of the Cathedral and occupied by nuns. One of the sisters had heard noises on the roof and this was the reason for the call to Scotland Yard. What followed was the most thorough search ever carried out by any group of officers in the Met. Once we had established there were no suspects on the roof we insisted we search all the bedrooms before we gave the all clear. We came across nuns dressed in all sorts of ways, some who screamed and some who were quite entertaining. It was certainly one of the most enjoyable searches made by a Wee Free of the Church of Scotland.

One of our watering holes was the Duke of York in Victoria Street. The pub was next door to the Victoria Palace where the famous and long-running Black and White Minstrels were performing. We got to know a lot of the cast, and a colleague, Pat MacGoohan, married one of the singers.

After I joined the CID, Pat McGoohan and I were posted to the Q car. We were in the Harrods area of Knightsbridge. My attention was drawn to a man carrying a large and heavy rug. I decided to stop him. Pat used to say to me, 'Jock, you pull everything that moves! What's wrong with this fellow?' Anyway, I decided to stop the geezer, who was not at all happy at being questioned. There was something not right about him that I couldn't put my finger on, so I decided to arrest him. The station van was called to take the prisoner and the rug back to the station.

The man was none other than Mickey Ball, a member of the Great Train Robbery gang. He had nicked this very expensive carpet, valued at £1,000 – a lot of money in 1968 – from Harrods. I think Mickey was more worried about what the rest of the gang would think of him getting nicked for such a petty offence as shoplifting. Mind you, by that time the rest were doing thirty years or were on the run.

Prior to the Great Train Robbery, the gang had carried out an armed robbery at Comet House, London Airport. This was the administrative offices of BOAC (British Overseas Airways Corporation) now British Airways. They were all dressed as city gents. They attacked the security van and stole £60,000. Several members of the gang were arrested, including Mickey Ball, who was one of the drivers in a getaway car. He was the only one convicted, and he got five years. Police believe this robbery financed the actual Great Train Robbery. Had Mickey not been arrested for that offence he would most definitely have been on the Train Robbery itself.

The next time I rubbed shoulders with one of the Train Robbers was many years later when I was posted to Kennington. Buster Edwards had a flower stall by Waterloo Station, and he and his stall became one of the tourist attractions in London. Buster frequented the Waterloo Hotel, just across the road from his stall. He liked a drink – a large brandy was his favourite tipple. I was in his company many, many times, and tried to cultivate him as an informant without success. Buster was excellent company, as were many of the heavies I have nicked. Sometimes I was in danger of forgetting the company I kept and how easily I could have got myself in trouble. It was important these underworld figures knew where they stood with me. I never gave any favours and they never asked any of me.

Sarah Churchill, Winston's daughter, lived in Eaton Square just up from the station. She was pretty fond of her whisky and she often drank in our own favourite watering holes, the Prince of Wales in Elizabeth Street or the Duke of Wellington ('Boots') in Eaton Terrace. When Sarah had one over the score she was extremely aggressive towards anyone and everyone. Most times she ended up being arrested. Once in the station she would strip off all her clothes before being sent to the cells naked. She was the most difficult person to control, but once sober, she was as good as gold. I became friendly with her porter, an Irishman. He gave me an old set of wine glasses that belonged to her which I kept for years just to tell people where they came from. They were just cheap glasses, used, I suspect, for a garden party.

I was patrolling Lupus Street one night when I came across a man lying in the gutter. I established his name was Jet Harris of the famous band Cliff Richard and the Shadows. He was completely legless but totally different from Sarah Churchill. Jet was a complete gentleman. He had recently split from the Shadows. Had he lived nearby I would have escorted him home. I couldn't leave him in the gutter, so I had to arrest him. He duly appeared at Bow Street Court and was fined the usual ten shillings. He thanked me for looking after him. I was sorry to hear that he had died in March 2011.

Imperial College Wages Van

I happened to be in the station one day when a man came to the counter. He was telling the station officer he had just come from Prince Consort Road which runs past the Imperial College. He saw a Group 4 cash-in-transit van driving past and heard three men who were standing on the pavement saying, 'Fuck it, we missed it!' He was able to give me the registration number of the car they got into.

I made enquiries with Group 4, and they confirmed that one of their vans had made a delivery at that time to Imperial

College. The car the men were in was stolen. The Detective Inspector, Mick Maidment, was off for the day, so I told the first class sergeant, who in turn told me he would lead an operation for the following week. He posted himself in my comfortable Q car, a beautiful Humber Super Snipe, while he posted me in our clapped-out Commer observation van. The sergeant warned me if the same team turned up I was not to arrest until he gave the order to do so over the radio.

Sure enough, the same team did turn up in the same stolen car and followed the Group 4 van into Hyde Park. At this stage they clocked us and made off. We gave chase in the observation van as I had decided there was enough evidence to arrest and charge them with conspiracy to rob. The radio was blaring, with the sergeant shouting, 'Abort, abort, abort!' We took no notice of him and arrested the whole lot. They were indeed a professional team of robbers. I had an almighty row with the sergeant when I got to the station – he was livid because I had gone against his instructions. But when I gave my evidence to the DI he just said, 'Charge them, Jock.'

The surname of one of the robbers was Van Dongen. He was living with his mother in the East End of London. When we went in to search his house his mother was sitting by the table, having just finished her dinner. There were two empty plates on the table. I asked her, 'When did you last see your son?' She replied, 'He's just left, that's his empty dinner plate.' When I told her he had been in custody for the previous four hours, her reaction was, 'I wonder who ate his dinner, then?' This was a typical answer from an East Ender.

Van Dongen and his team were charged and appeared at court the following day. They were bailed to appear at a later date. The following week the same team were arrested for robbing a building-site wages van on Rochester Row Police Station's patch. Some sergeants definitely get it wrong! This was one of many disagreements I had with senior officers.

A Week on the Throne

My family connection with the Throne is quite unique. In 1969, when the first Scottish National Party MP was elected, the Labour government of the day were afraid the Stone of Scone in place under the Throne would be stolen. It had been stolen in the 1950s by students, and recovered in Arbroath Abbey. This theft was investigated by Superintendent MacGrath, a Special Branch officer who was the previous tenant of our house in Sutton, Surrey. Several students were arrested for this crime, one being Kay Matheson who in later life happened to become my niece's teacher in Dingwall, Scotland. Senior police officers together with Government officials decided the Stone should be guarded during the hours of darkness. Detective Sergeant Mike O'Neil was in charge of the Aides to CID at Gerald Road, and he suggested the fairest way to assign officers was for us to cut the cards. John Batey, a Welshman, and I lost the draw.

Our hours were 8 pm to 8 am. Westminster Abbey is a graveyard and is not a pleasant place to be at night. We had no lights except torches, and there were birds flying all over the place, not to mention rats, mice and I suspect ghosts in the shadows, although I cannot say I ever saw one. It was still daylight when we went in to start the observation, so we were able to have a game of cards. I took a half-bottle of 'Johnnie Walker' in every night, and can honestly claim that Johnnie Walker and I looked after the Throne and the Stone.

One night there was a service on, and unknown to us it was being recorded for radio. Halfway through the vicar came over to enquire if we were talking. I had just lost a good cribbage hand to John, and all my swearwords came out on the recording. Years later when Windsor Castle went on fire it suddenly dawned on me that John and I had had no way of escaping from the Abbey, and had a similar fire happened there we would have been burnt to death. A few years later the supposedly valuable stone was returned to Scotland in the back of a pickup truck, without any security arrangements whatsoever.

Dips and Other Thieves

People who engage in pickpocketing are referred to as 'dips'. It is a very difficult crime to detect as they work in teams. Two engage in the actual theft by distracting the victim, while another two keep lookout. It is hard to get close enough to them to see what they are up to and get sufficient evidence for an arrest. They can also detect a plainclothes officer from miles away. The West End, Knightsbridge, Chelsea and Victoria are areas particularly attractive to dips. Ladies who shop around here carry thousands of pounds of cash and expensive jewellery in their handbags.

The Plummer brothers were black men actively engaged in pickpocketing. They also knew both Peter Upton, my 'buck' (which was what we called our partner), and me. This made it twice as difficult for us. We spotted them in a bus queue obviously at work and we managed to find an observation position on the first floor of Bayswater House, just in time to see them dipping their first victim. Next came the difficult part, as once they spotted us they would take off. Sure enough, they did.

Fortunately both Peter (a rugby player) and I were fairly fit. The brothers stopped a taxi and jumped in. We were close enough to stop the taxi, but they jumped out the other side and ran towards the Albert Hall, hoping to lose us in the crowds. Next they commandeered a London Transport bus. We managed to board it although it was still travelling at speed. Passengers were screaming as the driver feared for his life. We soon got the situation under control and arrested them. These active dips were wanted in police stations all over the West End of London. Luckily we were not injured and we received a Commissioner's commendation.

Peter Upton was my partner for a few years. We had many good jobs together and were commended several times for our work. One of our informants told us parking meter attendants who collected cash from the Westminster City Council meters were pocketing a lot of the cash themselves. The City Council were not aware of this. We set up a surveillance operation to catch them at it. After we had followed them for a couple of weeks, we got enough evidence to make arrests.

This operation took place at the time President Nixon was visiting the UK, in February 1969. Peter was not a qualified police driver, but in view of the fact he had been following the suspects on foot most of the morning, I took a chance and asked Peter to drive our unmarked van for a while and I would take up his position on foot. This, of course, was a disciplinary offence, but anyhow, off he went just as the Nixon cavalcade was moving away from the American Embassy. The unthinkable happened. Peter stalled the van in the middle of the road – panic stations! The police motorcycle escorts jumped off their bikes and bodily lifted the van onto the pavement with Peter still in the driving seat. We were expecting the sack that day, but Traffic Patrol clearly forgot to take the number of our van, as that was the last we heard about it.

Later the same week we caught all six attendants sitting in the back of their van. They all had their peaked caps on the floor filled with shillings and sixpences. After their arrest we went to search their homes. Our CID car was an A60 Cambridge estate. As we crossed Lambeth Bridge one of them asked where we were going. I told him we were going to search his house. He replied, 'You won't get the money I have into this car.' Sure enough, we had to turn back and collect the station van when we found he had three suitcases full of coins.

The men duly appeared at court and were sentenced. We estimated they had stolen £52,000 – a lot of money in 1969. Every council in London was after us to set up a similar operation for them, but our Chief Superintendent refused to let us go.

South Africa House and the American Embassy

During the late 60s there were huge demonstrations at South Africa House against apartheid in South Africa and at the

American Embassy against the Vietnam War. The demonstrators were well organised, hostile and violent. MPs, church leaders, students and members of the public were all involved.

One evening there was a big demonstration at South Africa House. I was not there but Mike O'Neil, my sergeant, was. One of the main instigators was seen throwing coins. Pennies, or any coin for that matter, can cause serious injury. Unfortunately, Mike was unable to get close enough to arrest him.

A couple of weeks later, when President Nixon was in Britain, there was another big demonstration at the American Embassy. This time I was there with Mike and John Batey. Mike recognised the culprit who had been throwing pennies at South Africa House and asked me to come with him to try and arrest him. We made our way into the crowd and got our man. This incensed the demonstrators, who attacked us, making a determined attempt to release our prisoner. Fortunately a uniform PC, Cyril Wheeler, recognised my mop of ginger hair and came to our rescue, together with several other colleagues.

As we were making our way toward the police coach with our prisoner, I looked behind me and saw that John Batey was dragging another man by the hair. I said to John, 'What have you got him for?' He replied, 'I have him for assaulting you.' But when we got to the coach John's prisoner shouted, 'For fuck's sake! Let me go – I am Special Branch!' I couldn't stop laughing. There is a retired Special Branch officer floating around who must be pretty bald by now, but I have never seen him since.

Sergeant O'Neil and I ended up in the Queen's Bench Division Court with our prisoner, and we can say we now have a 'stated case' to our name (i.e. a court case used as precedent for deciding other cases). We arrested our man for possessing an offensive weapon at South Africa House some two weeks beforehand, but the court ruled we could not arrest him if he was not in possession of an offensive weapon *at the time of his arrest*. He was found not guilty of possessing an offensive weapon but guilty of assault. I have a few press cuttings of this demonstration, including one newspaper picture of our future commissioner Sir Kenneth Newman being kicked in the face.

BOAC Air Terminal Robbery

In 1969 British Overseas Airways Corporation (now British Airways) had a terminal in Buckingham Palace Road. It was attacked by a team of robbers and a large amount of cash was stolen. Fortunately, no shots were fired and no one was injured. The team were well dressed and made good their escape. Mick Maidment was our Detective Inspector, who I would say was one of the most thorough investigators I ever worked for. He also had an excellent team in his office, including Sergeant O'Leary, Sergeant O'Neil, Pat McGoohan and Dick Gregory. A couple of days later, one of the vehicles used in the robbery was found abandoned in the Kennington area of London. When the car was searched we found a telephone number. This led us to several addresses which we searched with negative result, although some of the cash was traced to a post office in Kennington. We eventually found out the team had flown to Jersey, together with their families.

When police in Jersey were informed, they soon traced the robbers to a hotel on the island. Mike O'Neil and another couple of lads flew over to Jersey and identified the team. The hotel was raided during the early hours and a total of 14 were arrested, including women and children. The main robber was sleeping in a first-floor bedroom, and when two of our lads jumped on him the bed went through the ceiling and landed on the floor below!

Arrangements were made with customs for special clearance at London Airport. Every child, every woman, every robber and every CID officer carried a bottle of duty-free whisky for the thirsty officers left behind. The two main robbers were a Johnny Dark and Terry Millman. They all appeared in court and were sentenced to long terms of imprisonment.

A few years later, Terry Millman escaped from prison. He was circulated in the *Police Gazette* as being wanted. One day I was driving home from court and was stopped at a set of traffic lights in Croydon. I happened to look at the car alongside me, and who was sitting in the driver's seat but the bold Terry Millman! He recognised me and took off. Terry was driving a high-powered car and was getting the better of me, but I managed to call India 99, our helicopter. They followed him from the air to a house in Coulsdon. I searched the house but he was nowhere to be seen until I opened the trapdoor to the loft. There he was with a knife in his hand. He handed me the knife and said, 'Jock, had it been any other copper I would have used it.' This was one of several occasions when I had luck on my side.

Terry was a hardened criminal who had spent most of his life behind bars. He was still an active robber 30 years after we sentenced him for the BOAC robbery. In 2000 he was part of the team which attempted the biggest heist ever in this country. They planned to steal the world's largest perfect diamond from the Millennium Dome, but they were captured by Detective Chief Superintendent Jon Shatford and his team of Flying Squad officers. Jon and I served together on the Drugs Squad. Jon Shatford wrote an excellent book, *Dome Raiders*, about the case. Terry Millman died of cancer whilst still in custody awaiting trial for this robbery.

Brighton Train Robbery

Victoria Station, like any other busy railway station, attracts criminals such as pickpockets, thieves who steal suitcases and those who commit indecent assaults. The toilets in Victoria Station were a meeting place for gays who spent their time importuning. Peter Upton and I spent a lot of time patrolling the station looking for thieves (not importuning!). We knew every face, both male and female, who were of note, and we made many arrests for every type of offence.

One day I was reading the *Police Gazette* when I noticed the description of a suspect for a robbery on the Brighton train. The robbery had taken place in Brighton and the suspect's description was circulated by Brighton Police. I immediately recognised the details of a well-known villain who frequented Victoria Station – five foot, medium-to-stocky build, short curly hair, wearing blue jeans and with a dot tattooed on his right cheek. There were not many of that description, especially the height and the tattoo.

We telephoned Brighton and gave them the name of the person we thought was responsible. Brighton officers told us they had already interviewed him but had to let him go through lack of evidence. The following day Peter and I saw our suspect in Victoria. As soon as he saw us, he headed in the opposite direction, but we arrested him and took him to the station, where we interviewed him at length. He eventually made a statement under caution admitting the robbery in Brighton. Sussex police were informed, and didn't they look pretty sheepish when they came to pick him up!

My First Murder Squad

The headlines in the *Daily Express* dated Wednesday, 20 September 1967, read as follows:

> **CHELSEA PYJAMA GIRL MURDERED**
>
> A French girl was found murdered on her bed in a Chelsea flat yesterday with love letters and pictures of boyfriends scattered round.
>
> The flat is on the fourth floor of a house in Walpole Street, not far from the King's Road, centre of the so called 'Swinging London' scene.
>
> In the streets mini-skirted girls of many nationalities were stopped by police and asked if they knew the blonde from No. 17 called Claudy Danniel.
>
> She was sprawled across her bed, wearing only a pyjama top, when she was found by the landlord of the flats, Mr. Lawrence.
>
> Dr. Donald Teare, Home Office pathologist, could

not find a definite cause of death. But he told detectives he found bruises round the girl's neck and mouth. It is believed she was either suffocated or strangled.

Detective Chief Superintendent John Bailey, head of No 1 district CID, took charge of the Investigation.

In the flat detectives found last week's copy of the *Chelsea Post* in which a full-length photograph appeared of Claudy Danniel with two other girls in a beauty competition.

The girl used her two Christian names as a photographer's model. Her surname was being withheld last night until her family identified her.

Pictures of herself in low-cut dresses and bikinis were found among the 200 letters scattered round or stacked in drawers and cupboards.

Four detectives were detailed to sift through the letters. Most appeared to be from English boyfriends, but many others were obviously from friends in France. A score of photographs of men were also examined.

Last night twenty detectives fanned out from murder headquarters into the discotheques and clubs clustered around the King's Road. They believe Claudy Danniel was known in some of them.

More policemen, working in pairs, called at every flat and bedsitter in Walpole Street. They showed pictures of the girl – one was in a pouting Bridget Bardot pose – and asked 'Have you seen her in the last few days?'

Several of the bedsitter girls talked of men prowling the area at night.

At No. 17 there are two signs on the doorbells indicating the offices of 'International Tours' and 'American Adventure Tours'. Guarding the house were a uniformed Constable and a plain-clothes officer.

It is believed Claudy Danniel came to London from the Paris area in July. A friend said 'She was very sweet but typically French – a bit hot-headed at times.'

Claudy Danniel Delbar was her full name. Her death certificate states that she died from 'suffocation following cerebral haemorrhage and blows to the head'. This was an extremely interesting enquiry. Peter Sellers lived next door, and he was interviewed along with other celebrities of the time. We arrested an American by the name of Robert Lipman, who was convicted and sentenced to life imprisonment for the murder.

Throughout the enquiry I was paired off with a Sergeant. He taught me the importance of taking a detailed statement and the methodical way of writing it. Statements taken from witnesses in murder cases are very important.

Murder of Albert Charles Cox

Albert Charles Cox was found murdered in his flat at 7 Moreton Place, Westminster, in February 1970. The cause of death was 'asphyxia due to gagging'. Cox, born in Aylesbury on 18 August 1900, was a retired night porter and a homosexual. The murder office was based at Rochester row Police Station.

Our enquiries revealed that the Pimlico area of London was a haunt of homosexuals. Victoria Station was a central meeting point for gays. There are two army barracks in the area, Chelsea and Wellington barracks. Statements taken from many people suggested that squaddies attached to these barracks were in the habit of picking up homosexuals and robbing them. Usually they took the victim to either Hyde Park or St James's Park, where they attacked or robbed them. We set up observation posts in both parks, but during the period we kept observation there were no robberies reported. However, it was an eye-opener when one saw what happens at night in these two parks.

Several members of our team were asked to frequent known homosexual pubs and clubs in the West End with a view to gathering information on the murder. One night Roger Byrde, an experienced Sergeant and the oldest member of the murder squad, took four of us up the West End. We entered the White Bear in Piccadilly Circus, where we spread out at different tables.

Roger was about 55 at the time and an ex-paratrooper. Shortly after he sat down at his table he was approached by two men who were obviously soldiers. They asked if they could sit with him, and were soon in conversation with him. They suggested he bought them a drink, and Roger willingly did so as they continued talking to him. The rest of our team were in stitches.

After a while they got up and said to Roger 'Are you coming with us?' Roger replied, 'No, you are coming with me.' They said 'No, no, no. You are coming with us.' At this point Roger had had enough. He stood up and said, 'You are definitely coming with me tonight,' and arrested them. We guessed Roger had had enough by that point. They spent three days in custody but had to be released through lack of evidence. However, this certainly proved that squaddies were in the habit of trying to pick up men from West End pubs.

Peter Upton and I were instructed to interview Wilfred Brambell of the famous *Steptoe and Son* TV show. Our appointment was for 10am on a Sunday morning. He was up and waiting for us with a bottle of gin. By his own admission he was gay, but I cannot for the life of me see how he managed to get a partner. He certainly was not the prettiest face I have seen. He was also an alcoholic, and in my opinion a lonely man. We finished the first bottle of gin, then a second bottle. Around 1.30 pm the telephone rang and he answered it. It was our Detective Inspector enquiring if we had kept our appointment. Give him his due, he covered up for us and told the DI we had just arrived. I took a statement from him which I could hardly read myself the following morning. I felt sorry for the typist who had to type it.

The Escort Club in Pimlico Road was an upmarket gay club, frequented by well-known celebrities and royalty. One night while we were still on the murder squad I had arranged to meet a few of our team there – Peter Upton, Pat MacGoohan, Mike O'Neil and Roger Byrde. I arrived there a few minutes before them. As I entered the club a transvestite went up on the stage and started singing. He chose to sing a song I had never heard of, 'The Laughing Policeman', and as everyone knows most of this song just consists of the singer laughing. I thought he was taking the piss out of me. I got hold of the owner, who was a retired bank manager, and made him close the club. He was trying to explain to me that this was a very popular song, but I didn't listen to him. I was ushering the punters out of the club and on to the street when the rest of my team arrived. They thought there was a fire or some sort of emergency. I told them 'The bastards are taking the piss,' and explained to them what had happened. They creased up laughing, and assured me there was such a song. After I apologised to the owner, the club was re-opened and everything was back to normal. After a few drams I ended up on the stage myself, singing,

> I've just come down from the Isle of Skye.
> I'm no very big and I'm awful shy.
> All the lassies shout och aye!
> Donald, where's your troosers?

As I sang the last line all the 'queens' in the club started shouting, 'Get them off, Jock! Get them off, Jock!' I was always welcomed in the club after that.

The murder of Albert Cox has never been solved. We never even had a suspect. It is very disappointing for a murder squad when we don't get a result. I have been on many murder cases and this is the only one I was on that was never solved.

Burglars and Thieves

We received information that a team of burglars were going to break into a house in Ennismore Gardens, Knightsbridge. The information was quite specific, including the detail that they were going to get in via a skylight window. Paul, our Detective Sergeant, Phil, John and myself were going to wait inside the house for the bandits to enter.

The house, occupied by an elderly couple, was beautifully furnished with expensive antiques, valuable paintings and tapestry.

We told the couple what was supposed to happen and we took over the top floor. There were two bedrooms on this floor, one with two single beds, the other with just one single bed. As the night dragged on, we decided that, since we were near enough to the skylight that we would hear any attempt to enter, we might as well have a lie down. Unfortunately one of us had to sleep on the floor.

Paul and I bagged the two single beds. John grabbed the other single bed and Phil had to lie on the floor beside him. Everything was dead quiet, but I was still awake half an hour later when there was a hell of a commotion coming from Phil and John's bedroom. Phil, who had a squeaky voice anyway, was shouting and one could hear that he was struggling with someone. Both Paul and I were out of bed in a flash. It was still dark but we could see two men struggling on the floor. Phil was shouting 'He's jumped on top of me, he's jumped on top of me! Get him off!'

When we switched the lights on John was on top of Phil, who was trying to push him off. Poor John was as stiff as a plank and frothing at the mouth. He had suffered an epileptic seizure and fallen out of bed on top of Phil. Phil got the fright of his life, and no wonder. Once John came round we assisted him down the stairs just as the old couple emerged from their bedroom to see what was happening. They thought John was a burglar and they were delighted we had caught him. They even wrote to the Commissioner to thank us. The real bandits never actually turned up. A lot of time is wasted on jobs like this, but they still have to be covered. It doesn't matter where I am or who I am with, but whenever I think of that night I cannot help myself creasing up laughing.

An MP was robbed of his gold pocket-watch and chain in Hyde Park. Three of us, John Fassum, Peter Upton and I, were posted on night duty in the park to catch the robber, should he strike again. It was daylight at 7 pm when our shift started, so we decided to have a couple of beers in the Hilton Hotel. Peter bought the first round, which was three bottles of beer, costing something in the region of £6. This was away back in 1967 and I certainly could not afford to buy a round at that price. We decided to leave, but before doing so we ate all the free crisps and nuts that were on the empty tables. We had a drink in another bar in Park Lane. If the truth be told we were not too concerned about the MP who was robbed. What he was doing late at night in Hyde Park is anyone's guess. Hyde Park is a fascinating place at night, where you see all shapes and sizes, male and female, all colours and races, lying flat, standing up, front to back, back to front and bent over.

We came across two males with their trousers round their ankles, obviously performing an indecent act. I had a powerful seek-and-search torch, which I shone on them while John and Peter went to question them. All of a sudden one of them took off with his trousers still round his ankles. John gave chase, dodging in and out of the trees. I still had them both in my sight with the torch but John failed to catch his man. Peter and I couldn't stop laughing when John came back breathless. All he managed to say was 'Fucking wanker!' We debated if the man he was chasing was the MP who had been robbed of his watch.

Gerald Road was an excellent working station, but its one drawback was having to do boring postings when members of foreign states arrived. Sometimes this meant just standing outside a building or patrolling it for security reasons – in other words, being a glorified security guard.

One day Alastair McNichol, a young Aide to CID, and I were posted to a Commonwealth Conference that was taking place somewhere around St James's Park. I didn't fancy doing this, so on our way I suggested to Alastair that we go via Victoria Station to see if we could arrest someone. This would give us an excuse to avoid attending the conference. We were making our way down Eccleston Street when we came across a group of twelve kids. We decided to stop and search them. I couldn't believe my ears when they admitted escaping from a remand home that morning. Alastair and I were in luck. This would certainly save us from having to go to the Commonwealth Conference, and we marched all twelve back to the station. The charge room was packed, and because some station officers don't like being put under pressure, instead of being congratulated we got a bollocking for not going straight to our posting.

Victor Lissak was a practising solicitor with offices close to Bow Street Magistrates' Court. He was in court every morning, as indeed I was. He knew all the CID officers worth their salt by their first names. He certainly knew the thief takers, and indeed the thieves, as all or most prisoners coming to Bow Street Court would come to him to represent them. His first job was to apply for legal aid on the prisoner's behalf. This was of course a good earner for him. Mr Lissak was hard worker himself and would join us on night duty in the Q car to see how we operated. If any of us were on holiday or went a few days without a prisoner at court he would question the reason for this.

Years later I was on the Regional Crime Squad and had a prisoner at Kingston Crown Court. By this time Mr Lissak had been appointed a Crown Court Judge. I knew my prisoner was appearing before him. By this time of my service I knew all the defence counsels in central London. The same ones always represented the top criminals. I also got to know their good and bad habits. One particular one without fail asked to see your pocket book when you were giving evidence. I had written my notes in this case, but when I saw Mr Lissak was sitting I nipped into the police room and rewrote them all in Gaelic. Sure enough, counsel asked to see my pocket book. He looked and looked and studied my writing, but could not make head nor tail of it. Eventually His Honour Judge Lissak asked to see it for himself. I could see a smile breaking over his face. He looked at me and asked, 'Is this Gaelic, officer?' I said, 'Yes, Your Honour.' Defence counsel didn't ask any more questions regarding my notes.

We had some great characters as judges. There was one in particular about whom many stories were told. One of these is about a time when he was sitting at Inner London Sessions. He was about to sentence a prisoner and asked him, 'Do you want to say anything before I pass sentence on you?'

The prisoner replied under his breath, 'Fuck all.'

The judge then asked the defence counsel, 'What did the prisoner say?'

The defence counsel stood up and replied very slowly and deliberately, '"Fuck all", My Lord.'

'That's funny – I could have sworn he said something,' the judge commented.

Escorting a Prisoner

A prisoner I had arrested for robbery had jumped bail and failed to attend his court hearing. I circulated him as 'wanted'. When he was subsequently arrested in Glasgow, I flew up there to escort him back. As I was walking down Argyle Street on my way to the police station where the prisoner was detained, a car stopped and the driver shouted, 'Lemon, what are you doing in Glasgow?'

I thought, 'Who the hell knows me here?' The driver jumped out and there was Bo Bo, a local character from Stornoway. Bo Bo thought I was still in the Merchant Navy and asked what ship I was on. When he heard I was now a police officer he couldn't believe it. I told him I was picking up a prisoner and catching the 5 o'clock plane back to London.

I agreed to join him for a pint in Dick's Bar on the Broomielaw, the well-known watering hole for seamen and ex-whalers when I was in the Merchant Navy. Dick himself was in the bar, and he asked me if I had been a whaler in the past. When I confirmed I had been, he said, 'You bought the biggest round that has ever been bought in this house.' I wasn't surprised considering the amount of money I spent in Glasgow when I left the whaling.

This led to more and more drams and further and further into the afternoon. I telephoned Glasgow Police and asked them to deliver the prisoner to the airport, which they readily agreed to do. Bo Bo, being Bo Bo, promised me the airport was only 20 minutes away. Unfortunately he forgot to tell me they were constructing the M8 at the time. We got stuck in a traffic jam and just made it in time. When we got to the airport I was told by Special Branch the plane was waiting for me. The Special Officer was no other than Donald Stewart, who originally came from my village on the Isle of Lewis. He was able quickly to sort out the paperwork and we were ready for the off.

After I had handcuffed myself to the prisoner he refused to fly. One can make a prisoner travel by train, bus or boat, but regulations state you cannot make them fly. I asked him if he would fly if I bought him a half-bottle of whisky, and he couldn't get on the plane quick enough. I made it with the prisoner by the skin of my teeth. It didn't take long for the two of us to finish the half-bottle. This of course was totally against regulations.

Sutton and Croydon 1970-72

I left Gerald Road on 3 August 1970 and returned to uniform duties. Donalda was pregnant with our fourth child, Donald. She was hospitalised for six weeks and I managed to get a transfer on compassionate grounds to a station nearer my home – Z Division, which covered Croydon, Sutton and Epsom.

I was amazed at the difference in attitude between officers at an outer London Station and an inner London Station. During refreshments in the canteen they all switched off their radios so they would not be disturbed. They were older PCs than me, but as far as I was concerned their behaviour was not acceptable. I always left my radio on and was out like a flash should there be a call. I was not the flavour of the month with them. When one night a PC switched off my radio, I got him by the throat and told him if he ever did that again I would strangle him with the cord. No one ever challenged me after that.

Peter Kirk, a Scotsman attached to Sutton, was an excellent thief taker. He knew the ground inside out, and we soon struck up a partnership and exchanged information. Peter had a good informant who told him a man named Archie Campbell, together with a second man, was planning to break into Grant's Furniture Shop in the High Street. When I did some checks on Campbell I discovered he was a man I had arrested at Gerald Road some weeks before, and was actually circulated as wanted by me.

I informed John Pole, the CID Sergeant. We kept observation on the premises until midnight when the CID called it off. I asked Pole for permission to carry on with the observation on my own, but he refused and ordered me home.

I had only been at the station two weeks and no one really knew me. Who was I, already organising a team of CID and uniform to do an observation? On reflection, I don't suppose I blame him. I was absolutely fuming, but unknown to him I returned to carry on with the observation on my own. About an hour later Archie and his mate turned up, forced a side window and entered the shop. Both bandits were captured loading property into their van.

I submitted a report for the informant to be rewarded for the information he supplied. (I still have a copy.) This type of report was always done by a CID officer, so John Pole was not too happy. Allegations had been circulating for years that CID were claiming money for informants but pocketing the cash themselves. No wonder I was getting up their nose.

Archie Campbell was given bail again but failed to turn up at court for a second time. Two years later when I was stationed at Kingston my first arrest was Archie Campbell. One day whilst I was walking across the market in the centre of Kingston I saw him working on the roof of Woolworths. He was eventually sentenced for the outstanding crimes and on his release he emigrated to Canada.

Fred Jarvis was a Superintendant on A division when I was there. He was transferred to Sutton at the same time as me. Fred was a good senior officer for all the troops.

I was on the Q Car when he called me to his office in Sutton. At the time a lot of pubs were being converted to steak houses, with Berni Inns among the first on the scene. Fred told me that the manger of the brand new steak house opposite Sutton Station was having trouble with a team seeking protection money. 'I will leave it all to you, Jock,' he said.

I met the manager the same evening, and we were having a drink in the downstairs bar where he started to tell me what was happening. He had not got very far when he was called upstairs by the barman. The next thing I know, a man came running down the stairs two at a time.

I jumped up thinking this was a suspect. I gave him the best uppercut I could throw and knocked him sparkers. The manager then came down. He was not too happy, and said, 'For fuck's sake, Jock, that's my assistant manager!'

I just thought, 'Oh, shit.'

Little did I know then that the team who were putting the frighteners on the management was run by none other than Joey Pyle, who in latter years became one of the most sought-after targets in the Met. Joey was a criminal feared by all in South London. He was associated with the Richardson Torture gangsters and had mafia connections. I spent many, many hours following him, as did many other squad officers. The Met spent millions trying to arrest him, before he was eventually captured and given a long term of imprisonment. My everlasting regret is that he was not at the end of my beautiful right-hander that flattened the poor assistant manager.

I was again commended for the arrest of some housebreakers. My arrests brought me to the notice of Ken Ethridge, the Detective Chief Superintendent at Croydon. He asked me back to rejoin the CID as soon as my wife was fit.

Croydon is a busy town. The population at that time was estimated at 1,000,000 during working hours.

Lennie Lee was a convicted burglar who was wanted for similar offences when I arrived. He also had jumped bail. I had information that he was getting married at Croydon Registry Office, which was just across the road from the old Croydon Police Station, and the Registrar confirmed this.

Lennie turned up with his wife-to-be, together with the wedding guests. I waited until they were all inside, then crossed the road and arrested him. We had quite a scuffle with him and the guests, but I managed to handcuff him straight away. Suffice it to say we came to an arrangement that he could get married providing he agreed to remain handcuffed to me. We posed for wedding photographs with me as best man before taking him to the station. Lennie duly appeared at court, pleaded guilty and was sentenced.

Crime was beginning to escalate in Croydon during my time. New Addington Estate was a new estate on the outskirts of Croydon built to rehouse families from South East London. Many of these families were made homeless during the war, and had grown up surrounded by criminals. The estate became a breeding ground for crime. Drugs and glue-sniffing were causing problems.

I kept myself busy. Colin Burch and I searched anyone and everyone we suspected of drug offences, hence the reputation we got. We soon got our name in a local underground paper, *Red Fist and Bust*, under the heading 'Bust News'. It reads,

> THE TWO PIGS INVOLVED IN THIS HARASSMENT ARE DETECTIVE COLIN BURCH AND HIS PARTNER 'JOCK' (RED-HAIRED AND HEAVY). THEY ARE USUALLY IN THE 'RAILWAY' SO WATCH IT!

One day I was on the Q car with Malcolm Davidson, when we saw a van that was well overloaded and decided to stop it. It was full of brass fire sprinklers. The driver could not or would not give us a reasonable explanation for his possession of them. He was obviously on the way to a scrap-metal dealer. We took him to Croydon Police Station where he was interviewed at length, but he refused to answer any questions. The sprinklers had serial numbers on them, and we found out they were the property of a company called Automatic Fire Alarms.

I made contact with their chief security officer, John MacIver, a fellow Hebridean who had recently retired as a Detective Chief Superintendent from the Met. We arranged for John to come to Croydon to identify the sprinklers as the property of his company. He wrote a statement in which he identified the sprinklers by their serial numbers.

The suspect was charged with Handling Stolen Goods, and duly appeared at Inner London Crown Court, where he pleaded Not Guilty. The first witness was Mr MacIver and I was the exhibits officer, bringing along samples of the stolen goods. John was a big, broad man wearing a trilby hat and overcoat, the usual dress of a detective of his day. He was very impressive and professional in the witness box. I handed him a sprinkler which he identified as the property of his company. He was asked how he identified it, and he replied, 'By the serial number.'

The judge asked for the exhibit, which was handed to him by the usher. Having spent some time examining it, the judge eventually asked the usher to fetch his magnifying glass from his chamber. This was handed to him and he closely re-examined the exhibit. 'Mr MacIver,' he said, 'I have made every effort to find a serial number on this exhibit, but so far I have failed to find one. Can you help before I pass it on to the jury?'

I wished that the floor would swallow me. I realised I had handed John MacIver a sprinkler that didn't have a serial number. I dug into the bag and found one with a number, which was handed to John and produced as the proper exhibit. As he passed me after leaving the witness box, I could clearly hear him hissing, 'You bastard! I will get you yet!' The following day a bottle of whisky arrived on his desk.

Throughout his service John had served north of the Thames. He only ventured south of the river when he visited his daughter Joan. He always maintained all South London police officers were 'useless'. That day I had gone some way towards proving his point.

The subject of exhibits reminds me of the judge who thought he knew everything. He was dealing with a drugs job and one of the exhibits was a phial of heroin. The judge asked to see it and carefully examined it. 'Yes,' he said, 'It looks like heroin.' He then removed a small cork from the phial and sniffed its contents. 'It smells like heroin,' he concluded. He then held it to his lips and tasted it, saying 'Yes, it tastes like heroin. Where was this exhibit found, Officer?' The officer replied, 'In the anus of the accused, My Lord.'

The Spend-a-penny Robbery

The report in the *Croydon Advertiser* on 2 April 1971 was as follows:

> Police at Croydon are convinced that a local man played a vital part in the getaway of the armed gang who ambushed and robbed a Security Express van in Purley Way on Friday.
>
> They believe he choose the changeover point where £450,240 – a cash theft thought to be second only to the amount stolen by the Great Train Robbers – was speedily switched from a green van used after the hold-up to three other cars.
>
> It was just after midday on Friday that the biggest-ever cash robbery in Croydon took place at a lay-by in Purley Way, near the old airport.
>
> The raid sparked off the most intensive manhunt since the Great Train Robbery. A total of 200 detectives have been working on the case.
>
> They have swooped on hundreds of addresses in South London, seeking information about the eight bandits who took part in the ambush.
>
> It is possible the thieves have fled the country – but not by any of the orthodox airline or seaport routes because a security check was imposed before the gang could have reached these places.

Another theory is that they are hiding out in an isolated farmhouse somewhere in Surrey or Sussex – just as the train robbers did at Leatherslade Farm.

Two helicopters with police observers on board were out all day on Tuesday scanning part of the country for the three vehicles used by the gang in their getaway. But they found nothing and the search was not resumed.

Meanwhile the special robbery squad set up at Croydon assisted by officers from the Yard's Flying Squad, Regional Crime Squad and county forces, have descended on hundreds of addresses. At least 20 men have been interviewed at the Croydon headquarters.

'We have a number of useful leads,' said Chief Supt. Martin White, who is leading the hunt. 'It is a slow painstaking job sorting out every scrap of information.

We have set up a mobile police HQ at the scene of the robbery in Purley Way and are hoping that today motorists who use that route regularly will remember something significant about last Friday and contact us'.

A reward of £50,000 is being offered and this has no doubt accounted for the hundreds of telephone calls to the Incident Room say the police.

'Some of the calls have been from cranks, but the others have been checked out,' said Mr White.

The robbery took place when the security van stopped in a lay-by in Purley Way to enable one of the four guards to go to a public lavatory across the road.

The gang, one with a shotgun and all wearing masks, were hidden in a maroon van also parked in the lay-by. Two peep holes had been bored in the rear of the van so that the bandits knew when to strike. The bandits took just three minutes to unload 28 kit bags full of banknotes into a green van. 'The unloading usually takes security express men seven minutes but I suppose it was a labour of love for the bandits,' said a detective.

The four guards were locked in their van while the bandits drove off down Purley Way in their own van. They drove into the depot at Sleepeezee Ltd. There in full view of the railway line they switched the money into three cars, a red Jaguar, a blue Corsair and a green Cortina. They drove away and just disappeared.

Detectives are convinced a local man arranged the changeover point.

This was one of the biggest robberies of the time. A couple of weeks afterwards we reconstructed the actual robbery with Shaw Taylor for his 'Police 5' television programme. I was posing as one of the robbers, and I can say it took us a minute more to unload 28 sacks than it did the robbers. We never arrested anyone for this robbery. I believe it was an inside job, and after having spent weeks and weeks on the operation I was disappointed with the result.

Murder of Bill Goldsworthy

William John Goldsworthy was aged 79 when, at 3.15am on 18 October 1972, he was found dead by his grandson on a footpath opposite the church where he had been a part-time verger for the past five years. The footpath runs off Croydon Road, Wallington, Surrey. It is recorded on his death certificate that he died from 'cerebral contusions and lacerations, and compound fracture of the skull'.

This brutal crime was reported as 'The first mugging murder in London'.

Mr Goldsworthy had no enemies. He was well liked in the neighbourhood and by regulars who drank with him in his favourite pub, The Plough in Beddington. Mrs Alice Whinnett, wife of the landlord, said, 'He was a dear old chap and we knew him well as a regular.' He had lived in the area for the past 50 years, and although he was nearly 80 he was still fit and healthy.

Mr Goldsworthy left the pub at closing time to make his way

home via his usual route along the footpath running alongside Croydon Road. The path was not well lit, and has trees on both sides. He was later than usual in coming home, so his grandson went to look for him. He was horrified to find him covered in blood.

Detective Chief Inspector Micheal Hyans set up a murder office at Wallington Police Station. About two days after the murder we had the names of two suspects. This was followed up with observation points being mounted on several addresses. By the end of the week we were in a position to carry out some raids. As a result we discovered that the two suspects we were looking for were making their way by bus back home to families in Ireland.

We had little time to act. It was decided to stop all coaches on the motorway that were heading towards Holyhead. After a couple of hours we had a call from Preston to say they had arrested our suspects. Four of us went up to Preston in two Rover 3.5 saloons. I remember Eddie Goldsmith was one driver and Malcolm Davidson also accompanied us. We were delighted with the Preston officers who made the arrest, and to show our appreciation we suggested they join us for a pint. We went to a local club where we plied them with drink.

As we left Preston Police Station with the prisoners we spotted the crew of a local traffic patrol car coming into the station. They asked the desk sergeant who we were. We decided it was time for us to put our skates on. As we made our way towards the motorway, Eddie Goldsmith said, 'We have blue lights following us.' I told him to put our blue lights on and to put his foot down and head for London. The local patrol had Volvo estate cars. We left them standing in our Rovers and gave them a V-sign as they disappeared on the horizon.

William George Challis and Thomas Nolan were subsequently convicted of this murder. Several members of their families were also convicted of lesser offences.

Mistaken Identity

Reports were coming in of indecent assaults on passengers coming off the last train into South Croydon. Roy Painter and I were asked to patrol the area to catch the culprit, but we had little or no description to go on. We parked our car by some houses close to the forecourt of the railway station with the car windows open. As the last train was approaching the platform, a VW Beetle car came round the corner at speed. The car stopped, the driver jumped out and headed toward our passenger side where Roy was sitting. He grabbed Roy by the tie and tried to pull him out through the open window. I was sitting in the driver's seat absolutely pissing myself. Through his half-choked throat Roy managed to splutter 'We–we–we are police!' and tried to show his warrant card. The man tore it up and broke two of Roy's fingers.

After a minute or so I noticed Roy's face turning blue. I thought I'd better do something so I got out and said to the man, 'We are police, so just piss off or you're nicked.' At this he let go of Roy and gave me a beautiful right-hander on my cheekbone. Up to that day I had never arrested anyone for assaulting me as I always gave as good, as I got. When he gave me a second punch on the same cheek, I grabbed him by his lapels and gave him a Glasgow kiss which didn't do his nose any good. He was arrested and charged.

The following morning he was a different character altogether, full of remorse. He was employed as a bar manager of the Fairfield Hall, Croydon, an extremely good and responsible job which he would lose should his bosses find out he had been arrested. I managed to avoid telling the magistrate where he worked, so the press were not able to report it. This saved him his job. David was grateful and became a good friend. Every Christmas my family had tickets to watch the Christmas pantomime from the Royal Box. He was still, of course, the bar manager – need I say any more?

David was a bad, bad man with drink. He always gave me a few bottles for our Christmas party. One year when I was on the Regional Crime Squad, we had the Christmas party in the Greyhound pub in Carshalton, and David came as usual with his contribution. He got pretty drunk and was getting to the awkward stage. As he lived in Croydon, in the same area as Mike O'Neil, our Chief Superintendent, I asked Mike to drop David off at home. Off they went, and all was well until Mike stopped at the first set of traffic lights. Then, and for no apparent reason, David attacked Mike, who eventually managed to sling him out of the car. I was summoned to the Chief Super's office next morning, and when he told me the story I burst out laughing. He was not amused.

In 2009, 40 years after this incident, I called at the last known address I had for Dave Roberts. His wife Kathy answered the door. She did not recognise me at first, but then said, 'Oh yes, you were a detective, you took us to one of your police dinner and dances. My, you used to be good-looking!' I just replied, 'Do I look that ugly now, Kathy?' Sad to say, David was in a wheelchair and suffering from Alzheimer's disease, and he didn't recognise me.

The annual CID Christmas party in our day was something everyone looked forward to. Many guests, businessmen, publicans, solicitors, bank managers, and many other members of the local community were first introduced to each other at a CID party. It was frowned on by some officers, and as far as I am aware such parties are now banned. When I was scrounging in pubs for booze for the CID Christmas party, most publicans would ask what it was all about. I used to say it was a bring-and-buy sale – you take a bottle with you and at the end of the day you end up buying the bottle back.

The Christmas Club was something else. Nearly every pub, certainly in the outer areas of London, had a Christmas Club. These individual clubs were formed by the pub regulars, and every Friday after pay-day the punters, and in some cases the families, paid in their weekly contribution. By Christmas-time some of these clubs had saved a huge amount of money, often in excess of £20-30,000. This money was usually paid out in cash about three weeks before the festive season so that it could be used for buying presents. The treasurer always made contact with the CID to arrange for an escort from the bank, and to be present when the money was counted into individual packets ready for the punters to collect. This was an all-day job for us, although I shouldn't really call it a job. As you can imagine, everybody sent a dram over to us, and by the end of the day a five-year-old could have pinched the money. It was quite hilarious really, but our presence was much appreciated by the members. I can say to my knowledge there was never a robbery at a club where we were in attendance. On the other hand I heard of clubs being robbed where they had not asked for police assistance.

The Half Moon Public House

The Half Moon Pub in London Road, Croydon, was a dirty, run-down pub frequented by Irishmen, and this at a time when the IRA were very active in London. It was not the kind of place to take the wife. I was aware that police officers never used it and I always tried to avoid pubs other officers used. The first time I went in I went straight into the public bar, the bar used by all the navvies, and ordered a pint of Guinness. I could feel all eyes on me as I announced to all I was a new CID officer attached to Croydon, and that I had been told this was the best pint around. I had another and another, and went on to the whisky. I asked if any of them spoke Gaelic, and a couple nodded to show they did. By this time I was everyone's best friend.

After a few weeks I was accepted and, to a certain extent, trusted, probably because I was a Celt who was able to keep up with their hard drinking. One day Chris Faraghue, the manager, whispered in my ear to keep an eye on a large warehouse across the road from the pub. He wouldn't tell me why. 'Just keep an eye on it,' he repeated.

I did this over a period of time, noting the registration numbers of cars and trucks entering and leaving. I identified all the men and women concerned with the running of the warehouse and discovered they were convicted fraudsters. This was far too big a job for me to handle on Division, so I gave the information to C6 (Fraud Squad). Julian Bennington and his team took over the job and arrested several people for a £50,000 'Long Firm Fraud'. I knew after this that I had been accepted by the Irishmen. That was the start of a very long relationship with the Half Moon.

During the early 70s three Regional Crime Squad Officers were arrested, charged with serious corruption offences and convicted, in a case widely reported as 'The *Times* Enquiry'. I knew two of them. After they were sentenced, CID officers from all stations in South London arranged a fund-raising evening which was billed as 'The Catford Greengrocers' Association'. The money collected was to be given to their wives. Tickets were distributed to CID officers throughout South London, who then sold them as best they could at £5 per ticket - quite a lot of money in 1970.

Chris, the manager of the Half Moon, bought a ticket. We were going to go to the party together, but when I called for him at the pub he had already left. I ordered a drink and a man I had never seen before offered to pay for it. I accepted his offer and joined him in conversation. He was quite well-dressed for a customer in the Half Moon and I suspected he was up to something. Why buy me a drink, someone he had never met before?

He told me he was a lorry driver and I told him I was a publican and that I was waiting for Chris, as we were to attend a function later. He said, 'You are just the man I'm looking for.'

When I asked him why, he said, 'See that furniture truck outside? It's full of household furniture, and you can have it cheap.'

I went with him to the lorry, and sure enough it was full of brand-new furniture. I told him I would have to phone the wife first.

I went to the telephone-box outside and called the station. Bill Hucklesby, the DI, answered. I explained to him what had happened and asked him to send the Q car, but to tell the crew not to come into the pub. Bill (who ended up as a Commander) is the only colleague who never called me 'Jock', and to this day, with him, it is 'Mr Murray'. He just said, 'I'm sure, Mr Murray, you can look after yourself.'

I returned to the pub and told the geezer the wife was delighted. We had another couple of drinks and left. Both of us were well over the limit for driving. He did a three-point turn in the middle of London Road with his seven-ton furniture lorry. I kept telling him to keep an eye in his mirrors in case we were being followed by the 'Old Bill'. Meanwhile, the directions I gave him led us to the back yard of Croydon Police Station. His face went white. 'Fuck me!' he cried, 'Don't tell me you are Old Bill!'

My newly-acquired friend had earlier that day been given a start as a lorry-driver with a company in Bournemouth, having produced a stolen driving licence to get the job. The van was loaded up for him to do a delivery to Birmingham. The Half Moon was his first stop, and the first person he met was me. The following morning, when I was presenting the case at court, I could detect a smile on the Magistrate's face as he remanded the lorry-driver in custody.

I was pleased I missed the Catford Greengrocers' Association party, as the following Sunday there was a big splash in the *News of the World* about it. Senior officers were not too happy to read this, and for a change I was not involved.

There was a nightclub called Sinatra's in London Road opposite the Half Moon, with an Indian restaurant next door. The Indians complained of being racially abused by customers from Sinatra's, and several officers were sent to keep an eye on the situation. We got involved in a right punch-up with some yobs in Sinatra's. I ended up in hospital, but discharged myself about 4 am. Chris, the manager of the Half Moon, happened to be in the club and witnessed the fight. He actually saved my bacon by retrieving my warrant card, my jacket and one of my shoes. After I left hospital I drove past the Half Moon. There were several CID faces in there who were obviously discussing the evening's events and I joined them.

At that time the pub was being refurbished. The brewery gutted the place and made the three existing bars into one. A lot of money was spent on furniture and carpets. When I arrived in the bar I could see Chris was not too happy with the CID boys who were with him. The bar had a temporary partition while the workmen were doing the refurbishment on the other side. Chris in his temper put his fist through the plasterboard, in a show of strength I suppose, and cursed some of the lads. Neville MacAvoy, a CID officer and a fellow Irishman, said, 'So you think you are strong Chris? I can do that!' and he went wallop into the plasterboard, only to find there was a steel beam behind that section. That was the funniest thing I ever saw. Neville was in agony, and it didn't do his hand any favours.

Chris kept a donkey in the boiler room at the back of the pub. A down-and-out Irishman slept with this donkey. One night going into early morning, shortly after the pub had been refurbished, Chris asked everyone present (all CID officers) if they could ride a donkey. We all agreed there was no harm in trying. He fetched the donkey into the recently-decorated pub, and bets were made as to who could ride the donkey round the pub without falling off. The new carpet was to serve as a race track.

Chris agreed to give us a demonstration. As soon as he sat on the donkey it took off, and I mean took off! Chris went flying and broke his leg. That was the end of that little ploy.

I tell the following story to show the reader what devious, dangerous bastards a working CID officer sometimes has to deal with.

There were not many ginger detectives in the Met, and I think I knew them all. I was having lunch in a pub in Rotherhithe when a man approached me and said, 'You are obviously "Old

Bill" – are you Ginger Rogers?' (Not the actual name of the officer.) I knew the name he mentioned well. He was a serving senior officer.

I told him I was, and asked what I could do for him. He said his brother wanted to speak to me. He refused to give me the brother's name. I gave him my telephone number and told him to give me a ring. 'He won't meet you in a pub,' he said. I told him he could meet me in Southwark Park.

A few days later I had a call from the brother and that's where we arranged to meet. Jim Garlenge, our dog-handler, was in the bushes covering my back. The brother turned up at the appointed time and I introduced myself as Ginger Rogers. He told me who he was, but at the time it didn't mean anything to me.

The information he gave me was dynamite, all to do with the IRA and involving gun-running and drugs. It was something I could not handle as a divisional officer. I did a few checks on the man and found he was a well-known criminal. I arranged to meet the Detective Chief Superintendent on the Regional Crime Squad, who as it happened knew the informant. The information was so sensitive he wanted to form a special squad straight away, and I was to be included in this. A couple of weeks went by while we checked on some of the information he had given us.

There was an armed bank robbery in Kensington later on, where the robbers were ambushed by the Flying Squad. Shots were fired and a detective was shot. He was not fatally injured but received hospital treatment. When the dust settled down, who turned out to be one of the robbers but the very man whom I had met in Southwark Park.

A couple of years later I met Ginger Rogers, who by this time had become a very senior officer. When I told him the story, he just said, 'Serves you right for impersonating me.'

9

From Kingston to Scotland Yard

In 1972, after two years at Croydon, I was transferred to Kingston Police Station. Kingston is a lovely town on the river Thames, but it was too quiet for me. I was going further and further away from central London where I preferred to serve.

One day I had just come on duty at 9am and was having my cup of tea, when several men I didn't know entered the office. They confronted two of our Sergeants and took them away. Then they went to the Chief Inspector's office but he was not there. I thought, 'Bloody hell! What's happening here?'

Louis Moses, a first-class Sergeant, and I, were left to run the office on our own. I didn't have a clue what was happening, although I was aware that some of the officers had served on the Obscene Publication Squad (Porn Squad) and had been posted to V Division 'under a cloud'. A Chief Inspector, an Inspector, three Sergeants and a Detective Constable were all arrested from V Division. I had worked with these boys for several months and found them all to be excellent detectives. Apparently whilst they were serving on the porn squad they were corruptly accepting bribes and granting licences to porn shops selling dirty magazines. They subsequently appeared at the Old Bailey and were sentenced to long, long terms of imprisonment. It was a sad day for the Met.

I was off for the weekend and outside the house washing my car when my next-door neighbour came over with the *Sunday Express* and asked, 'What are you up to in Kingston?'

'Why, what have you heard?' I replied.

He showed me the paper, and there was an account of a minor job I had dealt with the day before. I had been in the office on the Saturday when a report had come in of a car making off from a petrol station without paying. This is a run-of-the-mill job, but as I had little else to do I went to the petrol station and took a statement from the forecourt attendant. I got the registration number of the vehicle concerned, which turned out to be a Morris Minor, but there was something about the witness that I was not too happy with. The owner of the car was traced and taken to the station. She was placed in the detention room until I had gathered all the paperwork, ready to interview her. I did everything by the book but did not charge her, because, as I have already said, I was not happy with the witness.

Shortly after my next-door neighbour left, the telephone rang. It was my Chief Inspector telling me the Commander wanted to see me straight away. There had been a complaint about the treatment of the suspect.

I went into the station and told the Commander what had happened and what I had done. His response was, 'I can't see why you didn't charge her.' When the complaint was investigated it turned out that the lady concerned was a relative of a *Sunday Express* columnist. I mention this story just to show how easily the press can get an officer, or for that matter, anyone into trouble. In fact I believe the suspect was innocent.

Stolen Car Squad 1974–76

My next posting was to C10, the Stolen Vehicle Squad at Scotland Yard. I was definitely going in the right direction in joining a specialised department at the Yard.

The Stolen Vehicle Squad was originally part of the Flying Squad, but as car crime was on the increase, in 1960 it was formed as its own separate department, with headquarters at Chalk Farm. In its heyday of the 1970s and 80s, the squad consisted of a Detective Chief Superintendent, a Detective Superintendent, a Detective Chief Inspector, four Detective Inspectors, twelve

Detective Sergeants, and 36 Detective Constables. They were supported by a dozen civilian staff.

The squad was very successful, and had a terrific reputation not only in the Met but with every other force in the country, who sent officers to C10 for training. Officers also came from countries all over the world to be trained by our squad. The motor trade was extremely supportive and we had a close relationship with them.

We dealt with stolen cars, stolen commercial vehicles, stolen plant, stolen caravans, stolen motor-bikes and stolen boats. We had a roving commission throughout the country. International and organised criminal syndicates are involved with the theft of vehicles and plant, which costs insurance companies millions and millions every year. I was very successful on this squad, but not necessarily in the recovery of stolen cars. I made arrests for drugs, robberies and cheque offences. In fact, I was so successful that Reg Lasham, our Chief Superintendent, reminded me I was on the Stolen Vehicle Squad and not the Flying Squad.

This was before the creation of the Crown Prosecution Service. In those days we were able to initiate prosecutions ourselves. We could arrange or object to bail for a prisoner. If I arrested a person for one or two stolen cars and he had a good solicitor, it was quite possible for him to get a Not Guilty verdict. In such cases I always gave them bail, on condition they would get me information about more serious crime, such as robberies, drugs or firearms offences. They always came up trumps.

Shortly after I joined the squad, three E-type Jaguars were stolen from a car front in Sutton, Surrey. I was assigned to the job. I found out who had committed the crime and actually recovered the stolen cars. For about two months I was seconds behind the suspect. Michael Fitzpatrick ('Ginger Mick') was a hardened criminal who was wanted all over South London for all sorts of crimes, including the theft of a couple of horses. I knew he frequented horse gymkhana shows at weekends, and so determined was I to catch Mick that on my weekends off during the summer, I took my wife and kids to these shows. My wife couldn't understand my sudden interest in horses.

During the period I was after him, he continued to steal expensive cars and committed several burglaries. I found out he had stolen a Jaguar XJ6 from the Croydon area and he was going to drive it to his friend's wedding in Hartlepool, where he was to be best man. I drove up to Hartlepool and found out where the wedding was to take place, but unknown to me, he had clocked me just as the wedding ceremony was about to start. He left the wedding and went to the dockside, where he put the stolen Jaguar XJ into gear, sending it flying into the water. I later recovered this car from the docks, but at the time I didn't know he was the one who had done this. I did find out he was heading back to London.

I contacted the motorway police and asked them to stop all XJs travelling south. This they did, but Ginger was not among the drivers they stopped. When I finally arrested him, he told me he had stolen a Land Rover and horsebox in Hartlepool and drove it to London. He could see the police were stopping all the Jaguars. Ginger Mick was eventually captured after a hectic chase around south London involving several of our cars. One of Ginger's victims (Ginger had stolen his horse) was in my car. The car immediately behind Ginger was giving us a running radio commentary on the chase. At one stage I didn't understand one message and I asked the victim if he had heard what was said over the radio. He replied, 'Yes, they just said he is heading towards my house with a sawn-off shotgun.' He then burst into tears.

Mick was finally cornered in a dead-end street. He and his mate made off into a school, which was promptly surrounded and searched. His mate was arrested, but we still couldn't find Ginger Mick. I was on the roof with Gilbert Lindsay, another DC on the squad. When we opened a skylight window, it was pitch black inside and all we could see was the barrels of a sawn-off shotgun pointing at us. Ginger was hiding in the photographic darkroom of the school. He gave up without too much of a struggle.

The following day he was put on an ID parade, in which he was picked out by the man who was in my car during the chase (the owner of the horse). As soon as the victim put his hand on his shoulder, Mick punched him in the mouth, knocking a few teeth out. His solicitor shook his head and said, 'I don't think you can deny that one, Mr Fitzpatrick.'

Mick admitted 42 burglaries, about 10 stolen cars and two stolen horses, as well as several counts of assault. He was sentenced to four years. I was commended by the Commissioner.

In December 2009, when I started writing this book, I tracked Mick down to an address in Croydon. He was pleased to see me and congratulated me on my determination to catch him away back in 1974. He told me he is still involved in crime, mainly shoplifting, and is earning a good living. Sadly, he is now addicted to drugs.

Stolen Paintings

I had information that a man by the name of Joseph Button, living in an address in Brixton Hill, was a receiver of stolen property. I was told he had several paintings of value in his house. Having obtained a search warrant, I met the rest of my team at Brixton at 7 am.

As we were about to knock on the door, Ian Brown, a DS on the Flying Squad, was coming out. Ian said, 'It's an Aladdin's cave, Jock. The place is full of rubbish, no chance of identifying anything.' I asked Ian what he had been looking for, and he said jewellery.

I thought the snout (informant) of mine had double-crossed me. He must have been working for the Flying Squad too. I thanked Ian, left the house and drove round the block until I was sure he had gone.

I went back to the house and my knock on the door was answered by Mr Button. I introduced myself and showed him my warrant card and the search warrant. 'The Flying Squad just left seconds ago,' he complained, 'they turned me upside down.'

'Tough!' I replied, 'I will have to do it properly.'

Ian Brown had told the truth – the place was absolutely chock-a-block with all sorts of junk. There was clearly no chance of identifying jewellery or any small antiques, but I thought paintings might be easier to spot. I was about to give up, but before doing so I had a last look on top of a wardrobe and found a painting of an apple, an orange and a pear. It didn't mean anything to me and I threw it on the bed. Mr Button shouted, 'Be careful – that's worth £100,000!'

I was gobsmacked, but I went on to find another three paintings. The total value was £500,000. Had Joe Button kept his mouth shut he would still be a free man. As it was, he went on to become one of my best informants before being shot dead some time later.

John Morrison and Other Officers

I mentioned earlier that there were always allegations against CID officers that they submitted reward reports naming bogus informants, and kept the reward money or part of it for themselves. The Deputy Assistant Commissioner (Crime) at this time, John Morrison, a fellow Islander, was determined to put an end to this practice, and insisted on knowing the true identity of any informant. When I submitted an informant's report as normal, giving the informant a pseudonym, it came back from Mr Morrison with a request for the informant's actual identity. I believe this was the first time ever such a request was made by the Yard.

I didn't have any problem naming my informant, but I thought, 'This is going to embarrass everyone at the Yard,' as in this case he was actually a senior CID officer who was on bail, awaiting trial for corruption. At the time serving police officers were not even allowed to speak to or contact him. I was left in an awkward position myself, wondering if I would be disciplined, but I heard no more about it. I could see no reason why I should not take on board information from this officer. In fact I reckoned he was a great guy to keep doing his job right up until the time he was convicted and sentenced.

John Morrison came from my village, and was the highest-ranking Met officer ever from the island. Just before John died in 2009, I went to see him. He was a man of few words. As we were having a chat over a dram, he said to me, 'You were sailing close to the wind when you were in the job, Jock.'

This really annoyed me and I replied, 'Are you suggesting I was corrupt, John?'

He said, 'No, not at all – I read all your informants' reports.'

It was only afterwards I wondered if he was referring to the above incident. I know John was worried in case I got myself in trouble. He never told me, but I strongly suspect he was behind my next posting to the Regional Crime Squad.

John Morrison was a senior officer who was very much respected by all ranks. He was the investigating officer on many major crimes both in this country and abroad. During the war he served in the Royal Navy and spent most of his service on the notorious Arctic patrol. John and his devoted wife Nan wrote a book, *Lewis and Harris Seamen,* in which they give a detailed history of seamen from the island who served in the Second World War. After he retired he returned to the croft, cut peats and was very much part of the local community. He never mentioned or boasted of what he had achieved.

Dave Cant was a Sergeant with me on the Car Squad, an excellent thief taker, a good interrogator and good in the witness-box. After having arrested two Irishmen who robbed a man of £500 using a sawn-off shotgun, at the station Dave was examining the shotgun and realised it was an expensive Purdey. He made enquiries and discovered it had been stolen some time previously and was valued at £32,000.

When the trial came up at the Old Bailey, Dave was cross-examined by the defence and the exchange went something like this:

Defence Counsel: 'DS Cant, did you call my clients cunts?'

Dave (looking at the Judge): 'I am afraid I did, your Honour.'

Defence Counsel: 'DS Cant, why did you call my clients cunts?'

Dave: 'Because I thought they were stupid.'

Defence Counsel: 'DS Cant, why do you think my clients are stupid cunts?'

Dave: 'Well sir, with due respect, what would you call anyone who cuts the barrels off a shotgun valued at £32,000 to do a £500 robbery?'

Defence Counsel: 'No further questions, your Honour.'

I met Dave at our reunion in 2010.

John Goddard was my DI at C10. He was an ex-Navy man whom I had never met before. He had been with us for about a week when I told him I had information about a yard in Sandwich, Kent, where I believed the occupants were heavily involved in ringing cars. John decided to come with me to have a look. We arrived there early afternoon, and we could see several cars being stripped. The yard was in open ground, surrounded by a 6-7 foot fence, with no place to keep observation. John asked me if I took a drink, and when I told him 'Just occasionally' (!) we retired to the pub and had lunch and a drink.

As time went on, conversation turned to our days at sea and drinks were flowing freely. John suddenly remembered it was Trafalgar Day, 21 October. The Royal Navy celebrate Trafalgar Day big time. John by this time was getting slightly lubricated, and suggested we stay down in Sandwich until it got dark, then we could climb the fence to investigate.

'It looks like it's a good job, Jock,' he said. Unfortunately, it was still British Summer Time and it didn't get dark until about 7 pm. By this stage John was anybody's.

We left the pub and made our way towards the yard. There was a large Alsatian dog growling on the other side of the fence.

John asked me to climb over the fence and have a closer look at the cars. I told him to fuck off. 'Don't tell me you are scared of a bleeding dog,' he taunted.

'Let's see you doing it, clever boy,' I replied.

John, at all times immaculately dressed, was wearing a three-piece, striped suit. Sure enough, he took off his jacket, handed it to me and climbed over. He was just about to let go of the top of the fence and drop into the yard when the dog appeared and came pelting over. He took a chunk out of John's striped trousers and, I suspect, his arse. He was back over the fence like greased lighting and landed in a heap beside me. I was still laughing as I drove back to London. He rarely asked me to go for a drink with him again.

When attached to specialised squads you work all sorts of hours, day and night. You might be following a team and all of a sudden something unexpectedly happens and a search warrant is urgently required. This happened to me on many, many occasions and in different parts of the country. If you needed a warrant during the day when the courts were sitting that was OK, but if one was needed in the middle of the night you had to seek the nearest JP.

All police vehicles have their own individual logbook, which shows the history of the car together with the mileage made on every trip, when it was last serviced etc. Whenever I went into a JP's house for a warrant I carried it with me. The JP would read the information for the warrant and ask 'Have you got a bible, Officer?' I would say yes and show him the logbook, which looked pretty much like a bible. I would lift it in my right hand and rattle off, 'I swear by Almighty God the evidence for this warrant is true to the best of my knowledge and that is my signature.' Most JPs, especially in London, never had a bible and I was never, ever challenged.

Shortly after my father-in-law died we were up on our yearly pilgrimage to Scotland. Both my parents-in-law were devout Christians, and grace was said before and after every meal. One day my mother-in-law, Annie, asked me to say the grace. I was taken completely by surprise, and while this was not the first time I had said grace, I just could not remember the words. I thought, 'Do I know anything with the word God in it?' Then I had a brainwave - I put my head in my hands and intoned, 'I swear by Almighty God that the evidence I give shall be the truth, the whole truth and nothing but the truth.' Annie was quite impressed until she saw my wife laughing and questioned her. We celebrated the 50th anniversary of C10 in October 2010. We were told the staff at C10 that year had been reduced to one Detective Inspector, eight Detectives, two vehicle examiners and an intelligence unit.

10

Regional Crime Squad 1976–1980

In 1976 I was posted to the Regional Crime Squad, whose terms of reference are the prosecution of travelling criminals, direct from the Stolen Car Squad. This was a prime posting and much sought after by all thief-taking officers. I had now joined the elite, and at first, based at their Mitcham office, I was slightly concerned as to whether or not I was a good enough detective to cope. Within a very short time I found my feet and was as good if not better than most of the team I joined. I certainly brought more work in than anyone else.

While absolutely delighted by this posting, I was a little surprised. Throughout the 1970s there were several trials at the Old Bailey involving officers attached to squads at Scotland Yard. Porn Squad, Drugs Squad and some Flying Squad officers were arrested and convicted at the Old Bailey for corruption. The then Commissioner ruled that all officers serving on squads had to return to division for at least two years before they could get posted back to the Yard. In my case I went straight from one squad to another. Altogether I did six straight years before going back to division.

Lorry Load of Tinned Meat

A lorry load of tinned meat was stolen from the back of Tesco in Wandsworth. One of my snouts told me part of the load went to a pub, the Wagon and Horses in Garratt Lane. I kept observation on the pub for a couple of days, and found it was doing 'afters' between 3 and 5 pm (pubs used to close between 3 and 5 pm in those days). I kitted myself out in bib-and-brace dungarees with 'New Century Window Cleaning Co.' emblazoned across the front, then went round a few houses nearby, signing up enough customers to start a window-cleaning round. When the publican of the Wagon and Horses also employed me for his windows I was welcomed for the afternoon 'shut-in'. I introduced myself as 'Bill the window cleaner'.

I stayed in the pub drinking with the other customers on the afternoon of Thursday and Friday. By then I was pretty positive, having seen the portions of cold meat on sandwiches and salads, that some of the stolen meat was on the premises.

I got a search warrant and at 7 am on Saturday morning I knocked on the pub door. The owner opened up, still half-asleep, and said, 'What the fuck do you want at this time of the morning, Bill?'

I replied, 'I am "Old Bill" today,' and showed him my warrant card and search warrant.

'I don't believe it,' he said, 'is this a wind-up, Bill?'

'I am looking for a large quantity of stolen tinned meat.' I went on, 'Have you anything like that on the premises?'

'No, sir,' he said. We searched the pub, and in the cellar I noticed a door partly hidden behind some beer barrels. I told him to open it. He said he had not been in there for years and claimed he did not know where the key was. I told one of the boys to get a jemmy from our van. The publican then decided he had the key and opened it for us, revealing the stolen meat. He was arrested.

Entrance to the cellars of pubs in London is usually via a hatch in the pavement. I told the team to park the van and I would throw the cases of tinned meat up to them. This worked OK until I came across a case that was heavier than the rest. I think it contained spam while the rest had corned beef. I went to lift it and I immediately suffered a hernia. My balls were down by my knees.

The van was pretty low on its rear wheels, and as one of the boys was driving it back to the station a rear wheel came off. We had overloaded it. The misuse of a police vehicle is a serious disciplinary offence, and any defects have to be reported to Traffic Patrol who thoroughly inspect the vehicle concerned.

I called a friend who had a truck, and we transferred half the load on to it. We waited until the truck was gone before calling traffic patrol. For once they were baffled and could not figure out why the rear wheel had sheared off. I was questioned at length, but they failed to get the truth out of me. I would guess they had a sneaking suspicion as to what happened.

The next thing was to search the publican's house in Wallington. On our way there he complained, 'It's not my week, Bill.'

'Why is that?' I asked.

'When I was out walking my dog a few days ago,' he replied, 'he shit on the pavement. This was witnessed by a copper who reported me. I appeared in court last Monday and I am the first person in Britain to be fined for letting my dog shit on the pavement.'

I managed to continue work for the next six weeks until I went to Sutton Hospital to have the hernia repaired.

Shortly after the above incident and before I went to hospital, our office were asked to give the Flying Squad a hand with early-morning raids throughout the Home Counties. We had to parade at the yard at 4 am. Chief Superintendent Mick MacAdam was in charge of the operation, and he gave a briefing to some 50 officers. Each team was given an envelope with details of the operation and photographs of the target they were to arrest. Mr MacAdam came to one envelope and he stood silent for a minute before he opened it. He took out the photo and said. 'I don't think we will send Jock Murray on this one.' He showed the photo to everyone present. There I was, bold as brass, coming out of the Burn Bullock public house with Brian Sangster, who was one of their main targets. Sangster and the rest of his team were nicked.

About a week later I was called to Sutton Hospital and I was in there for a week after the operation. During this period Sangster

R 675212 | 3 | SEAMAN'S RECORD BOOK AND CERTIFICATES OF DISCHARGE | 4

CRI 2/6 Paid

NAME

National Insurance Number	Union or Society
ZW/49/91/11/A	Name...... No......

Income Tax Code Number and Date

S 25/4/57

Pension Fund and Registered No......

DECLARATION.

I DECLARE (i) that the person to whom this Discharge Book relates has satisfied me that he (she) is a seaman and (ii) that the photograph affixed bearing my official stamp is a true likeness of that person, that the signature within is his (her) true signature, that he (she) possesses the physical characteristics entered within and has stated to me the date and place of his (her) birth as entered within.

Signature of Supt. at Mercantile Marine Office— J. Ogilvie

Date

R675212

M.M.O. Embossing Stamp

NAME OF SEAMAN.

*SURNAME (in Block Letters)	*CHRISTIAN NAMES (in full)
MURRAY	JOHN

*Delete for Asiatics.

Date and Place of Birth		Nationality
26-12-40	GRESS LEWIS	BRITISH

Height	Colour of Eyes	Colour of Hair	Complexion
5' 11"	Blue	Ginger	Fair

Tattoo or other Distinguishing Marks

Grade Number and Date of Issue of Certificates of Competency Held

B.S.I.C. Serial No. BS518554

N.S. (AF) Regn. No. or Service in Armed Forces

Signature of Seaman J. Murray

My Seaman's Record Book

New Year's Day, 1958, on the MV Hertford *going through the Suez Canal. All these seamen came from the Western Isles. (Left to right) Anthony MacNeil (Vatersay), Dougie Murray (Lewis), Murdo MacNeil (Barra), Murdo Gillies (Lewis), Murdo MacLean (Lewis), the Author and John MacLeod (Lewis)*

The barrel, where we would spend one hour off and one hour on, looking for whales.

All these men were from the Western Isles.

Catcher alongside the factory ship, with a whale being used as a fender.

Willie Macleod and me at an illegal 'still party'.

Alex MacKinnon, me and Jimmy Tulloch with flensing knives and boots for wading in the whales' blood. We are standing by a whale's tongue hanging on a derrick wire.

A bothan, an illegal drinking den on Stornoway used by whalers on their return from the sea. They were often raided by the police.

Geoff Watts, left, and me at Peel House Police Training School.

Peter Cameron in the No. 1 uniform which is now no longer worn.

Rehearsing for nuclear war – travelling with the Mobile Column in the early 1960s.

Me on the left handcuffed to Charlie 'Chopper' Knight, the leader of the armed robbery gang that we rounded up in Operation Ohio.

General Charlie gets £1·3m and 54 years

By WILLIAM LANGLEY

THE 'GENERAL' who plotted a £3·5 million raid on the liner QE2 stood in a dock yesterday, bowed to the judge and said: 'Thank you my lord.'

Charles Knight, also known as 'Chopper' and 'Top Cat' was being jailed for 21 years — the final instalment to a total of 54 years' imprisonment.

It was the last act in the story of his daring robberies, distinguished by flair, boldness and brilliant planning, that netted £1·3 million. Only £345,000 has been recovered.

A 15-man commando-style raid on the liner would have been the highlight in the career of the chain saw gang led by Charlie Knight, 34.

He planned a dockside snatch of millions of pounds worth of foreign banknotes being loaded at Southampton for passengers to spend at ports of call on the ship's world cruise.

But before the theft could be pulled off, the gang had been caught.

In one dramatic incident police chased Anthony Knightley, known as the 'Chain Saw Man' through road blocks at 60 mph. He drove into the sea at the Solent near Southampton, and swam away as police fired shots at him from the water's edge.

Three other men were with Charles Knight in the dock to be sentenced by Mr Justice Stocker at Maidstone Crown Court.

Terence Read, 40, David Bales, 33, and Alex Sears, 36—all described by the judge as dangerous and very intelligent men—were each jailed for 18 years to run concurrently with 15-year terms they are already serving.

They were being sentenced for a £96,000 raid on a security van in the Blackwall Tunnel beneath the Thames.

Knight and his men carrying shotguns, pistols, and an axe, and travelling in stolen vehicles, had forced an armoured Group 4 van into the tunnel wall and robbed it.

It was only after that theft that police got a lead on the Chain Saw Gang.

Det. Supt. Charles Snape, second in command of the CID in South-East London, had been called to the scene and eventually headed a team of 70 detectives from several parts of the country in an operation code-named 'Ohio'.

On December 6, 1977, when Sussex detectives interviewed a man about something else in Canterbury Prison, he asked to speak to Mr Snape, and told the superintendent he had heard two men boasting about several big 'jobs'. He named seven men.

Arrested

That information led to the setting-up of Operation Ohio with officers from Essex, Kent, Cleveland, the West Midlands, Thames Valley, City of London and South-East London.

The team was to collect dossiers on more than 44 robberies—at one time almost one raid a fortnight, including a £47,000 London toy factory raid, £78,000 from Rochester Post Office, and the chain-saw attack on a security van at Banstead, Surrey, that netted £788,000.

Police heard stories of tests carried out on cutting open security vans with chain-saws.

Seven days after the Banstead robbery, the chain-saw operator, John Segars, 31, was arrested and £34,000 recovered. He offered to talk.

A few days later in a police raid on a caravan site at Box Hill, Surrey, Samuel Benefield was arrested and another £83,000 seized. Benefield also 'grassed'.

Benefield, like Segars awaiting sentence, was 'The General's' first lieutenant. It was from him that detectives learned of plans to raid the QE2.

Knightley, 34, one of the chain-saw operators, was finally arrested by two unarmed policemen in Hythe, near Southampton. He has already been sentenced to 16 years.

Eventually Charlie Knight, a former painter and decorator, of Beale Road, London, E., was arrested after a chase through the East End.

In August this year he was sentenced to 18 years for the Banstead chain-saw raid. He was already serving 15 years for the Rochester Post Office robbery.

Newspaper coverage of Charlie's trial.

HOUSE OF LORDS

Margaret Thatcher

28th July 1999

Dear Mr. Murray

It was a joy to open your generous and historic gift of the first bottle of "The Whalers Dram" whisky.

I found your letter fascinating. Too few of our people know the brave and exciting experiences of those who fished in the seas around South Georgia. There is many a story that has never been told but which should be written before it is too late. The fact that we are a sturdy seafaring people has had a great influence on our character and therefore on our history. It certainly was important in recovering the Falkland Islands.

May I also add my thanks for your service in the Metropolitan Police, especially during the Miners' strike and the demonstrations at Wapping against the Murdoch press – two other battles that had to be won.

We have lived through a remarkable century and have never been defeated.

All good wishes

Yours sincerely

Margaret Thatcher

John "Jock" Murray Esq.

THE RT. HON. THE BARONESS THATCHER, L.G., O.M., F.R.S.
HOUSE OF LORDS, LONDON SW1A 0PW

The letter I received from Mrs Thatcher after sending her the first bottle of the Whaler's Dram whisky

With Donalda at the opening of The Whaler's Rest

was released on bail for receiving stolen cigarettes. The ward I was in was on the ground floor with patio windows leading to a lawn. The curtains were always drawn for the afternoon siesta but I always stayed awake. I could see some movement behind the curtains. All of a sudden the curtains were pulled and who walks in but Sangster with a present of 400 stolen cigarettes. What a capture from my hospital bed!

When I was discharged I asked the nurse how long should I refrain from having sex. The nurse reminded me of 'Keyhole Kate' in the *Dandy* comic. She was most definitely a spinster and I suspect a virgin. She replied, 'At least six weeks.' Two weeks later my dear wife informed me she was pregnant, and nine months later my little boy Alasdair was born, seven years after our last one.

Baptism with My Gun

My wife Donalda is a practising Christian, and we were married in the Free Church of Scotland in London in 1964. Shortly after we had our second child there was a dispute within the London church over the sacrament of baptism. Several members of the congregation were involved, and we decided we would leave and attend a church nearer our home in Sutton. This happened about 10 years before Alasdair was born. The minister who caused the problem had by this time left, and my wife wanted to go back to the London Free Church.

When the time came to baptise Alasdair I had to ask the elders of the congregation if we could have him baptised in the Free Church. They told me I would have to appear before the Church Session. I thought, 'That's no problem. I am at sessions every day of my life – Inner London sessions, Snaresbrook Crown Court, Kingston Crown Court and the Old Bailey.' Not exactly church sessions, but I looked forward to it just the same.

I was told to be at the YMCA in Tottenham Court Road at 7.30 pm on a Wednesday. I asked my DI, dear old Peter Simpson, if I could get an hour off. When he asked me why,

I told him I had to attend church. He burst out laughing and thought I was taking the piss. When I told him the reason, there was no problem.

There was a problem for me, though, because at the time we were following a robbery team. I had earpieces from two different radios in my ears. I was also carrying a gun.

I arrived at the appointed time and waited until 7.45 pm. No one came to see me. I was listening to my team through my earpieces as they continued tailing the robbers. Eventually I got up and opened the door. Three or four of the elders were sitting round a table, obviously discussing me.

'I was here at 7.30 pm as asked,' I told them. 'It is now 7.45 pm, and I am armed.'

Waving the gun at them, I continued, 'I cannot leave the gun in my car, and I am not supposed to be carrying it in public, so what's happening?'

Angus MacAulay, a lovely guy, said, 'We will be with you in five minutes.'

'I won't be here in five minutes,' I replied. 'I will wait for two minutes then I am off.'

Sure enough, Angus was out in a minute and told me I could baptise my son in the Free Church.

Years later the minister at the time, Jack MacLeod, was in hospital in Stornoway. He was telling this story to the nurses. When my daughter Catriona came on duty the nurses were asking her if she knew who the madman was who went to church in London with a gun, asking for a baptism. My daughter had to admit it was her father.

Charlie Drake

During the summer of 1976 I had a loft extension put on my house. The plans were made by a reputable surveyor, Bill Jenkins, who had been recommended to me by an old friend. Bill suggested I employ a builder he knew, who for the purpose of this book we will call 'Charlie Drake'. Charlie was a loveable rogue, but a good tradesman. I took two or three weeks off work to do the labouring for him.

One day Charlie Drake arrived for work and said, 'Do you know if a load of sewing machines have gone?'

I told him I didn't have a clue, as I had been off work for some days – why did he ask? He told me he could buy brand-new ones for £20.00.

I gave him £80.00 and asked him to get me four. The only reason I had so much money on me at the time was because the mortgage company had released money for the extension.

The following day he arrived with the sewing machines. If my memory serves me right they were battery-operated, but worth a lot more than £20.00. I traced them to Wimbledon Sewing Machines, and when I showed them to Ray, the Managing Director, he identified them as his property. He also said he was the sole importer to this country and that they were worth £120 each. He had stored them in an empty house in Haydons Road. As far as he was concerned the load was still intact.

We went to Haydons Road, Ray opened the front door and, sure enough, the room was packed with the machines. 'The load is still intact,' he said.

I asked if he had checked the rear entrance – he hadn't. When we did we could see a large empty space by the rear door. He couldn't believe his eyes. The only thing he said was, 'Shit! I'm not even insured.'

That same night I got a couple of our units to keep observation with me. At midnight one unit left, while my colleague, a little Irishman, and I stayed. At 1 am I was about to pack up, but decided to have a quick look down the alley to the rear of the house before calling it a day. As I crept alongside the fence I heard a slight noise. I stopped and looked through a small hole in the fence, only to find the villain looking straight at me through the same hole. As I jumped over the fence I got a brick in the head, but managed to arrest him. I got the prisoner to wake up the Irishman, who was fast asleep in my car.

Charlie Drake told me new furniture made by the long-established company, Myers Beds, was sometimes sold cheaply from the back of a lorry on the Roundshaw Estate. I traced the lorry, which belonged to Myers. I approached their directors, who were not aware they were losing any stock.

I followed the lorry for a couple of days and found the driver was dropping off furniture at stops not on his schedule. I eventually arrested him, and recovered numerous expensive items of furniture, including the dining-room suite presently in my home. When Myers had a stock-take they found they had lost £80,000 worth. I gave them advice on their security procedures which they implemented and is still in operation to this day. They offered me a private reward for my work which I refused, suggesting they send a cheque to a Police Orphans Fund.

I ran out of money before Charlie Drake finished the work on my extension. The last job to be done was tiling the new bathroom. I told him he would have to wait until payday at the end of the month.

I had just bought a new car and Charlie knew this. My old car, a Vauxhall Victor, was parked outside my front door. I was not using it and had intended to sell it. Charlie told me he would tile my bathroom if I gave him the Vauxhall in payment. The deal was done.

Two weeks later the local police called at my door. They asked if I was the owner of the Vauxhall. I told them I was not, as I had sold it a few days previously.

'The car is still registered in your name,' they said. 'Who did you sell it to?'

After I gave them Charlie's name and address, I also told them I was a serving member of the Regional Crime Squad and asked what the problem was. They then told me the car was involved in a smash and grab on a jewellers' shop in Coulsdon, Surrey. I couldn't believe my ears. Charlie was duly arrested.

Some time after he finished working for me, Charlie was stopped by a uniform PC for a Road Traffic Act offence. When it came to court there was a dispute over identification of the driver. The PC said in his evidence, 'I never forget a face once I have seen it.'

A few months later the PC murdered his wife, and during his trial he told the jury he could not remember where he had buried the body. Charlie read about this in the paper. He immediately appealed against his conviction for the Road Traffic Act offence on the grounds that, 'If the PC cannot remember where he buried his wife, how could he remember my face?' He got away with it.

My wife is a nurse and used to work in the local hospital, St Helier. A few years after our extension was completed, she came home one morning and told me the man who was working on our extension had been admitted to her ward and died. She was quite upset. When they went through his property they found a large amount of money he had hidden in his spectacle case. Charlie was a character, not always honest, but likeable.

Armed Robbers

One of our team had information that an armed robbery was to take place in the Queens Hotel, Crystal Palace. The information was quite specific – the bandits were going to tie up the night duty porter, take the keys to the safe and empty it. Two of our units, A and B, were posted inside, armed and hiding behind the reception desk. The rest of the team, some armed, were in various positions outside.

As two bandits arrived we radioed the units inside to warn them the robbers were on their way. Both men went straight into the hotel and out of our sight. Next thing we heard was a shot from inside the hotel. Shortly afterwards there was a second shot. We rushed inside and found one of the bandits on the floor. Our two units inside appeared to be OK. Apparently what happened was that Unit A stood up, saw a bandit putting his hand inside his jacket as if he was going for a firearm, and shot him. He then ducked back behind the reception desk and lay on the floor. Unit B thought unit A had been shot by the bandits. He then jumped up from behind cover and he also shot the bandit. In the confusion Unit A and unit B both thought the bandits had fired at them only to discover they were both OK. The robbers were overpowered and the wounded man survived.

Number 9 Regional Crime Squad covers the London area. We had five offices in London, based at Mitcham, Brockley, Hendon, Barkingside and a central office at Scotland Yard. Owen Phillips, a City of London Detective Inspector, was in charge of the Central Office. Owen wanted assistance with a team of robbers who were expected to rob premises in Hackney. Our team from the Mitcham office were to arrest the bandits when the signal was given to attack.

I was driving the nondescript van, and I parked it a couple of blocks away from the targeted premises. We sat listening on the radios to the progress of our surveillance team who were following the suspects. There must have been between six and eight officers in the back of the van.

When any squad is waiting for an operation like this to come off, everyone is tense and on edge. Each officer reacts in a different way. Some are bubbly, some are quiet, and some act completely out of character. As the driver I was in the front on my own. We listened to the radio commentary as the robbers approached the premises. All of a sudden one of the lads farted. This led to: (1) a howl of laughter, (2) shouts of abuse, (3) threats to throw him out of the van. The next call was Bill Forman, our DI, who was in another vehicle, coming over the radio shouting 'Go! Go! Go!'

I was immediately in gear and off at speed. When I got to the location all the boys piled out of the back door and into the fray. On jobs like this you don't park – you stop anywhere, jump out and do what has to be done. I always carried a pickaxe handle, especially when I was on an armed robbery job. It was much better and more effective than the issue truncheon. I was the last out of the van because I was the driver.

Knowing that the team we were following were all black, I grabbed the first black man in sight, arrested him and made my way back to the van, only to find I had forgotten to put the handbrake on. It had rolled several yards down an incline and into a wall.

I asked my prisoner, 'What's your name?'

When he answered, 'Joe Black,' I thought, 'Smartarse, you're definitely nicked.'

Once we got back to the station it turned out that my prisoner's name was actually Joe Brown. The poor fellow had just had a haircut in the shop next door, and happened to come out as the robbery was in progress.

Robbery of a Flat

We had information that two men were to commit a robbery, but we had no idea where. We knew where they lived and we knew the day they were to commit the crime. We were assisted by C11, a department at the Yard which specialises in surveillance and covert operations.

At 7am the bandits came out of their house carrying a 'happy bag'. This is what we called any bag carried by robbers, housebreakers or drug-dealers. They both got into a black taxi and set off into the middle of the London early morning rush hour. We followed them over the river, past Victoria, into Hyde Park Corner, Park Lane and on to Marble Arch. They finally stopped outside a block of flats in Portman Street.

Both men went inside, and we took it for granted they were to pick up another member of their team. Specialised squads like the Regional Crime Squad, Flying Squad and Drug Squads operated using channel 7 on our radios. Most uniform units used channel 1. We were sitting waiting for the bandits to come out when an urgent message came over on all channels: 'armed robbery in progress' – and the address given over the radio was the block of flats our targets had just gone into! It must be our targets committing the robbery.

The next thing we heard was police sirens, and suddenly there were flashing blue lights coming from all directions. Colin Bush, who was with me in the car, was armed. By this time the uniform lads had arrived and started fighting with our units, thinking we were the robbers.

Colin and I jumped out and ran into the flats. I was in front of Colin, who was shouting at me, 'Jock, stay behind the gun! Stay behind the gun!' It was part of our training never ever to go in front of the armed officer. I shouted back, 'If you shoot me, Colin, I'll fucking kill you!'

I have already mentioned that everyone acts differently in such cases. I thought I was invincible, which on reflection was stupid. I never gave it a second thought that the robbers might be armed. We took the stairs two at a time.

As we got to the top floor, our two targets emerged from an apartment door. The first target, Teddy French, had a gun and was pointing it at us. I was about three steps lower and level with his legs. I did a rugby tackle, diving for his legs, and he overbalanced and came tumbling down the stairs. It is difficult to explain to anyone how one reacts when faced with a gun. Every situation is different. I was able to disarm him and I don't think he enjoyed being dragged down the stairs to the ground floor by his hair.

Colleagues and Friends

When I joined the police, David Davies was a uniform constable at Gerald Road. Dave was a Welshman, dead keen on the job and a good socialiser. He was one of the officers who took me out learning beats. When David left Gerald Road he went on to C11 (surveillance) squad at the Yard. He also drove nondescript vehicles such as black taxis, Land Rovers and any of the numerous types of vehicles his department possessed. He was classed as one of the best operators in his department. 'Taff', as he was affectionately known, was extremely reliable.

There was an occasion when I was targeting a robbery team from the Streatham area and asked for C11 assistance. I had a name, Ray Fowles, and address for one of the team. My intention was to follow Fowles and hopefully identify the rest of his team so we could mount a proper operation.

This particular morning we were meeting at 6am. Everyone turned up apart from Taff. This was unusual, as he was always on time. We could not raise him on the radio and neither could his office at the Yard. It was 10am before we heard he had had an accident with his motorbike and was in hospital.

He didn't have a scratch on him and there was no damage to the motorbike, but he was paralysed from the neck downwards. I was absolutely devastated and called off the operation until our team had got over the shock. The galling part for me is that Ray Fowles was nicked by Detective Superintendent Tony Lundy and his Flying Squad team while they were 'across the pavement' on a robbery a couple of weeks later. Tony Lundy became one of the most successful officers ever at Scotland Yard. That bastard Fowles turned 'supergrass' and admitted numerous offences, as well as implicating many other criminals who were convicted on his evidence.

This did not help poor Taff, who was confined to a wheelchair and for the rest of his life had to be hand-fed by his devoted wife. On later occasions I was able to take him out to a few places such as Wimbledon for the tennis, but I felt terrible every time I came across him afterwards.

I have already mentioned that as a child I was given the nickname 'Lemon'. I tried my utmost to make sure none of my colleagues found this out. I was one day on the fifth floor of Scotland Yard. This floor was where all the senior officers of various squads had their offices. If a junior officer was seen there colleagues would immediately think you were sucking up to them for something. I was getting to the end of the corridor when I heard a voice shouting 'Lemon! Lemon!'

I just thought, 'For fuck's sake! He can't be calling for me.' I purposely didn't turn round and just carried on. The same voice shouted twice as loud, 'Lemon! Lemon! Come here, I'm talking to you.' By this time several senior officers had their heads out of their doors wondering what was happening. When I looked round there was Eddie Holbrook, the Chief Superintendent of the Flying Squad, laughing his head off. It so happened he was living next door to friends of ours from Lewis, and my name had come up in conversation. Thus my well-kept secret was revealed to the whole of Scotland Yard. The first Sputnik that went into orbit had a dog called 'Little Lemon' in it. I was referred to as 'Little Lemon' by many senior officers after that day.

My First Buy Job

One of our Sergeants, Jim, received information that some Irish gypsies had several guns for sale. There was a large colony of gypsies in the Woolwich area of London, some whom were heavily involved in organised crime. Jim suggested I go in and do the buy, as my accent was similar to Irish and I could speak Gaelic. This was to be my first 'buy job'. At the time the IRA were heavily involved on mainland Britain and were responsible for bombings, mostly in the London area. I had all this in the back of my mind.

The informant introduced me to two gypsies with thick Irish accents, naming me as 'Jock'. I decided not to try and change anything, just be myself and lob in a couple of Gaelic words here and there. They searched me first to see if I was armed. They didn't have the guns with them. After a bit of chitchat they decided I was OK. One of them whistled, and with that a third one appeared from nowhere. He had a loaded .38 revolver with him. I realised I knew very little about guns, and it taught me a lesson for the future: never get involved in buying anything, especially guns, drugs or jewellery, unless you are well versed in the particular item you are buying. We discussed a price and prices for other weapons they said they had access to.

My story was that I was an armed robber, with a speciality in robbing cash-in-transit vans. This was a serious problem in the Met at the time. I told them I had already shot a policeman and was wanted for it. They would not sell me the gun at the price I offered, but they promised to supply me with other types of guns. After we parted the gypsies told the informant there was no way they would sell guns to 'that headcase'. 'He's already wanted for shooting a policeman!'

I mention this because I had gone over the top with my ploy. It taught me a lesson. Little did I know that two weeks later I was to begin two years engaged on 'Operation Ohio', investigating armed robberies that involved cash-in-transit vans.

Going undercover is a specialised job and not for the faint-hearted. In my day there was no training whatsoever given, but nowadays there is a special department at Scotland Yard with experienced officers who just deal in undercover work. All recruits are highly trained and are excellent at their job. They have certain qualities and lots and lots of bottle. I really do admire the work they do.

11

Operation Ohio

Towards the latter part of 1977, there were a number of major enquiries being conducted by various police forces throughout the country relating to serious armed robberies in which vast amounts of money were stolen, and in several instances where people were shot and critically injured. At this time, there were no suspects and no concentrated liaison between forces. It must be said that the varying methods used by the criminals responsible suggested that several different teams were committing the robberies, and this confused the issue.

On 6 December 1977, a prisoner who was serving his time in Canterbury Prison asked to see Detective Superintendent Charlie Snape, who was later to become the operational head of Operation Ohio. He told Mr Snape that two inmates of the prison were boasting they had pulled off two major robberies, one on a post office in Rochester, Kent, and the other in the Blackwall Tunnel, London. He named other members of the gang as Charlie Knight, Sammy Benefield, Jim Moody, Alex Sears and John Woodruff. I shall return to the two above-mentioned robberies later in the book.

This vicious and highly organised gang of robbers were known as 'The Chainsaw Gang', because of their expertise in using chainsaws to cut the side out of security vans. They were also known as 'The Thursday Gang' because of robberies they committed on Thursdays on factory estates and steelworks in the Midlands.

On 1 June 1978, a meeting took place at Hatfield Police Station between senior officers in whose areas the armed robberies had taken place. It was unanimously agreed that a joint Provincial/ Metropolitan operation should effectively commence on 12 June. Officers from No. 5 Regional Crime Squad, No. 6 Regional Crime Squad and No. 9 Regional Crime Squad, together with officers from Cleveland, Kent, Sussex, West Midlands and the Met, were selected for the operation. Detective Superintendent Snape from the Met was placed in charge of Operation Ohio, with Detective Inspector Bill Forman, also from the Met, as his deputy. Both Mr Snape and Mr Forman were excellent leaders with a vast amount of experience between them. The No 9 RCS (Met) officers seconded to the operation all came from our Brockley office, and I was the only officer from the Mitcham office.

The operation was called Ohio because of the Cleveland officers, who suspected that the Thursday Gang had committed a robbery in Billingham, Cleveland. The famous American city of Cleveland is of course in the state of Ohio. As it turned out the Billingham robbery was one of the few crimes that the Thursday Gang or Chainsaw Gang did not commit.

Just before this operation was instigated, there was an armed robbery at Sainsbury's in Cheam, Surrey. I had information and the names of the suspects allegedly involved – Charlie Knight, Jim Moody and Alex Sears. I had drawn their Criminal Record files from the Yard and was preparing an operation to follow them. One day Bill Forman came into our office and asked for these files. I told Bill I was investigating the Sainsbury robbery and that I was in the process of putting an operation together. I refused to give the files to him. We had a bit of an argument and Bill left in a huff. At that stage I was not aware of Operation Ohio. Shortly afterwards I had a call from Mr Snape, asking me to come over to Westcombe Park Police Station, which was to become the appointed headquarters for the operation.

Mr Snape explained to me the reason for his request for the files, and let me know of the existence of Operation Ohio. He then invited me to be part of this operation. This was arranged with my bosses at the Yard, and I was delighted. I was to spend two exciting years on this operation, together with 53 other officers.

We were given a list of 20 targets, and from June until August 1978 our job was to house (i.e. locate) the main ones:

(1) 'Chopper' Charlie Knight, the leader of the team and known as 'Top Cat' or 'The General'.

(2) Sammy Benefield, Chopper's deputy, known as 'The Scotsman'.

(3) James Moody, the strong-arm man, known as 'Toggles and Chains' and 'Big Jim'.

The next few weeks were pretty tedious, keeping observation for hours, taking photographs, following targets and taking vehicle numbers, in an attempt to identify suspects, associates and suspect premises. After a short time it was evident we had a leak amongst our team. One of our observation posts was in a block of flats overlooking the Blackwall Tunnel. Our interest was in a yard close by. Two lanes of a motorway and a further two hundred yards of ground separated the observation post from this yard, but shortly after we were in position one of the targets was viewing our observation post through a set of binoculars. From then on everyone was looking over their shoulders. Operation Ohio lasted two years, and we were towards the end of it before we found out who the leak was. The suspect officer was arrested at a later date on a completely different operation.

Through various means at our disposal we found out that the team were going to hijack a plane which collected old Scottish banknotes once a month from all over the south coast of England. The plane carried around £2 million every month. They were going to attack it at Northolt Airport in North London and were already referring to it as 'The Great Plane Robbery'. We had all the targets plotted up and followed them to King's Cross, where they parked their vehicles and entered a small cafe. They had a meeting, probably the last meeting before the actual robbery. While they were inside the cafe one of them spotted a motorbike which they believed belonged to our surveillance team. It could have been any motorcycle, but that was enough for them to call the job off. This was a most frustrating day for us. We didn't know why they had called off the hijack until after they were finally arrested at a much later date.

On 15 August 1978, a Security Express vehicle was attacked in Sutton Lane, Banstead, Surrey. It was carrying three-quarters of a million pounds. Eight men, one (Jim Moody) dressed as a police officer, had faked an accident using six vehicles and a van, and when the security van pulled up it was immediately attacked by the robbers. They blew out the tyres of the security vehicle with two shotguns, cut the side out of the van where the safe was located with their chainsaw, and helped themselves to the cash bags. The robbers, their weapons and the bags containing the cash were quickly transferred to their own Sherpa van. They made good their escape through the grounds of Banstead Hospital, where they again transferred the load of cash, firearms and chainsaws into three stolen Ford Granadas and Cortinas.

Superintendent Snape and Chief Inspector Forman, together with some of the troops, went to the scene. After examining the vehicles and obtaining the description of the bandits and the method used, they were satisfied the team involved was that of our main targets. We believed this was the first job they had done since our operation commenced, and a more determined effort was made to trace them.

Arresting the Gang

Information was received from an informant (who had since been shot dead by police while committing an armed robbery) that John Seagars had travelled to Scotland after the robbery. However, Seagars and his family were traced to a guest house in Minehead, Somerset. Our office had circulated the registration number of a Range Rover we knew to be in his possession.

All the family were arrested. John Seagars was in possession of 14 pounds of cannabis resin and over £2,000 in cash plus the

Range Rover, which had been purchased for £4,500 from the proceeds of the Banstead robbery.

Seagars' family were questioned, and his wife Theresa disclosed that he had been involved in the Banstead robbery. Seagars himself refused to answer any questions and sat on the floor with his legs crossed like a Buddha. His mother and father, who were also arrested, admitted their son's share of the robbery proceeds was in two large suitcases at the address of another relation, Aunt Sally, in the Notting Hill area of London.

On 26 August a strong contingent of Ohio officers crashed into a house at 26 Droop Street, W10. We asked for Aunt Sally, and to our amazement the occupiers had never heard of her. We had raided the wrong house! Bill Forman and a couple of other officers were having a discussion as to our next step when a little girl came up to us and asked who we were looking for. Bill Forman told her we were looking for Aunt Sally, and asked her to go and find her. The little girl left and a short while later she returned and told us Sally lived in No 10.

When we knocked at No 10, the door was answered by a lady with an unlit cigarette in her mouth. When we entered she tried to light it from an unlit gas fire. She was obviously panicking. We asked her where the two big brown suitcases were and she replied, 'Up in the spare bedroom, under the bed.'

Bill Forman and some of our team went upstairs and found the two suitcases, which they carried downstairs. Bill forced them open and found they were stuffed full of bundles of £20, £10 and £5 notes. Aunt Sally said, 'Fuck me! I've never seen so much money in my life!' She then fainted. The contents of the suitcases weighed nearly half a hundredweight.

We returned with the suitcases to Banstead Police Station. The money was shown to John Seagars, who just threw up his hands and said, 'Fuck it – I've had enough!' By 10 o' clock that evening he had told us the names of the eight-man team on the Banstead robbery, the part each man played, the share-out to each member (£96,000), how they escaped, the vehicles used and the flop (house) used to share out the loot, which turned out to be Jim Moody's flat. We were all over the moon. The money in the suitcases was counted and came to £84,500.

We now knew the names of the entire team on the Banstead Robbery:

Charles Roland Knight, known as 'Chopper', leader and organiser

Samuel Thomas Benefield, Chopper's deputy

Anthony Knightly, brought onto the team with Khan because of their cutting experience

Bernie Khan

John Woodruff, strong-arm man for frighteners, to put the wind up the victims of the robbery

James Alfred Moody, impersonated a policeman for the robbery

Brian Sims, driver

John Seagars, our prisoner

The following day a statement was taken from Seagars in which he admitted the part he and every other member of the team had played in the robbery. We went over the getaway route used by the robbers with him. He told us he was with Jim Moody in a stolen Ford Granada, speeding away from the robbery scene with the chainsaws, guns and sacks full of money, when a police car with its siren blaring shot past them at speed going in the opposite direction. Seagars' bottle went, and he decided to get out of the car. He arranged with Moody that they would meet later at Moody's flat.

Seagars then went into the first public house he came across, where he bought a large brandy and a pint. When he put his hand in his pocket to pay for the drinks he felt a spent cartridge case which he had put there after discharging it at the scene of the robbery. He went to the toilet and hid the cartridge on the floor behind the toilet pan. When we recovered the spent cartridge from the pub toilet, this was the first corroborating evidence we found.

Seagars identified Jim Moody's flat to us and told us about an abortive attempt to rob a security van in the northbound lane of the Blackwell Tunnel on 4 March 1978. He also told us about their successful attempt, again in the Blackwall Tunnel, on 29 September 1977. This was the first time they had used a chainsaw.

Seagars was unable to tell us the whereabouts of the rest of the team. Because of the leak who we already knew was plaguing us, a second, false, statement was taken from him in which he implicated only himself. This was put into our filing system and the proper statement was kept safe with Charle Snape and Bill Forman.

A search warrant was obtained for Jim Moody's flat in Hackney. When it was established that no one was at home, the front door was forced. We found some cash bags from the Banstead robbery and also a crash helmet worn by Moody during the actual robbery. Forensic experts found the fingerprints of Moody, Benefield and Knightly in the flat.

A second member of the team, Sammy Benefield, was arrested on 29 August in his caravan at the Roof of the World caravan site, Box Hill, Surrey, together with his wife Edith. Members of our team had traced a Barclaycard used by his wife to purchase a meal in a restaurant in Chelsea. We recovered £82,994, the remaining proceeds of his share of the robbery.

Benefield coughed to the robbery straight away. He could not face a sentence of twenty or more years and wanted to do a deal with us. He confessed to a total of 45 offences he and others had committed throughout the country. He agreed to give evidence against his fellow criminals, which he later did. He did not find out that John Seagars had turned 'supergrass' until 20 December 1978, when Bill Forman told him. 'Fuck me, Bill! I can't believe it,' was his reaction. 'Anyway, John Seagars isn't in the same league as me. He is only a slag.'

Meanwhile our own troops were dispersed all over the Home Counties looking for the rest of the robbers. I was sent to Bournemouth with four or five others to look for Jim Moody and Tony Knightly, who we were told were staying in a caravan in that area. There are hundreds of caravans in the Bournemouth area, and it was just like looking for a needle in a haystack. We stayed there for a week with no result, and returned to London on 30 August 1978.

I was home for a couple of hours and had just settled down with the wife and kids. I had bought the kids a stick of Bournemouth rock each. We were about to have dinner when the phone rang. It was Bill Forman. 'Jock,' he said, 'Alan Walls [a Cleveland officer] and Ian Brown have housed Jim Moody and Tony Knightly in the Riverside Caravan Park, Hamble, Hants. Get as many guns as you can from Mitcham and we will meet you at Eastleigh Police Station.' I still haven't finished that dinner.

I got and signed for five guns from Mitcham Police Station. Regulations say you are not to take guns from one force area to another without permission of the Chief Constable or his Deputy. But when you were on a 'high' on such operations, regulations, as far as I was concerned, came second. I clearly remember Charlie Snape in a Ford Granada squad car driven by Chalky White, a Flying Squad driver, overtaking me on the M3. I was doing 100 miles per hour in my Volvo, so Chalky, who was some driver, must have been doing in excess of 120.

When we got to Eastleigh Police Station it was dark. Mr Snape decided to keep Moody and Knightly under observation until daylight. We were sure the arrest of these two men would involve a shoot-out. In the middle of a caravan park at night-time it would be too dangerous to the public to go ahead. We arranged to meet again at 3.45 am for a proper briefing, which would be followed by the hit on the two caravans involved at 5.30 am.

We established liaison with Hampshire Constabulary and while we were making these arrangements, Moody, for some unexplained reason, left the site before we were all in position. I still strongly believe that the leak within our team was responsible for this, although I have never had concrete evidence to back up my theory.

At 2 am Tony Knightly was also preparing to leave the site. He carried something heavy to the boot of his car and drove off. Our containment units were alerted to set up roadblocks about a mile away from the site, but Knightly smashed through the roadblock and drove on in his badly-damaged car. The engine bonnet had sprung open and he had to drive with his head out the passenger window. Without either Knightly or us realising it, he drove down a dead-end road leading to the beach. He abandoned the car on the foreshore of the Solent and was chased on foot by Ohio officers. As he left his car he turned round and pointed what we believed to be a weapon in our direction. Ohio officers immediately opened fire. We lost Knightly, or we thought we had, as he disappeared into the Solent. When his car was searched we found £78,000 in the boot.

Now the fun began for the officers concerned as far as the paperwork was concerned. The shit hit the fan for the following reasons: (1) Ohio officers had fired shots in Hampshire Constabulary territory. (2) We were carrying firearms in a different force's area without their knowledge, something which was frowned on. (3) We more than likely had shot, if not killed, Knightly. (5) I had taken and signed for five guns and taken them out of the MPD (Metropolitan Police District) area without permission. The station officer at Mitcham was also in the shit because of me. Instead of celebrating the arrest of two active robbers we were ourselves under investigation big, big time. We didn't know if we had shot Knightly at this stage. By this time BBC and ITV were aware of the shooting and it was also headline news in the national papers.

We were writing reports for the next two days. Luckily for us, later an old lady who had read the papers called us to say a man was acting suspiciously near her house. A car was sent to the area and there was Knightly, still dripping wet and waiting for a car to take him to London. It was a miracle he had survived the bullets fired at him and the fast-flowing tides of the Solent. After he was arrested he told us he never had a gun and no weapon was ever found. He had pulled himself onto a boat that was anchored in the Solent, where he stayed overnight before making his final swim ashore. At one stage he was nearly run over by the QE2, which, as it happens, was to be their next target after the Banstead Robbery. Apparently, in 1978, the liner carried £3,000,000 on board to operate its casinos.

Tony Knightly was a likeable rogue with a sense of humour. The whole squad really admired the effort he put in to avoid capture. In the car on the way back to London he confessed to Bill Forman his part in the robbery, but said he did not know anything about the money in the boot of his car. At his trial he claimed he was looking after the money for John Woodruff, a fellow member of the team, whose money we never recovered.

We maintained observation on the caravans, hoping Jim Moody would return, but he never did. We now know he had been on his way back to the caravan site when he had purchased a newspaper. The headlines told him about the police chase the previous night involving Tony Knightly and the shooting. Needless to say, Big Jim Moody made an about-turn back to London.

On 4 September 1978, Ohio officers made a determined but unsuccessful attempt to arrest Sims. He was seen driving his Jaguar, bearing the personalised numberplate BS 7697, and followed to his wife's address at the Guinness Trust Buildings, Stamford Hill, NW16. Two officers from Essex Constabulary, Graham Welch and Keith Bartlett, stepped out in front of his car and tried to stop him. They were lucky to escape serious injury as he drove straight at them. Graham Welch managed to get his hand on the driver's door but had to let go.

On Sunday, 17 September 1978, we received information that Sims would be at his girlfriend's address at 49 Sycamore Court, Chingford, E4. I was with Bill Forman and other armed officers who surrounded the address. As we entered, Sims appeared on the first-floor balcony dressed in pyjamas with his clothes under his arm. He was about to jump but he soon changed his mind when he noticed an armoury of guns pointing at him. He surrendered without any further trouble. His house was searched but no evidence relating to the robbery was found.

Sims denied any knowledge of the Banstead robbery. He also denied assaulting the two officers with his car on 4 September, stating it must have been his brother, who, as it happened, was the spitting image of him. I went with Liz Strachan, a WPC attached to our squad, to a garage at the rear of the flat, where we found a suitcase full of money totalling £86,048. Dear old Bill Forman was delighted.

When we arrived at Greenwich Police Station I interviewed Sims with Bill Forman. We showed him the cash and asked if there was any more of the Banstead robbery money. He fainted with shock – or something like that! When we revived him he confessed.

On 9 September 1978, we arrested John Woodruff (known as Big Bad John) at Manchester Airport as he stepped off the plane after his holiday in Malta. After two days in custody he wanted to do a deal and become a supergrass. He was told we had all the evidence we wanted, as a couple of his team had already turned. Woodruff had only recently been released after doing nine years of a 14-year stretch for armed robbery. He was sitting in the cell one day looking very down, and when Bill asked what was wrong he said, 'I feel such a big cunt, returned from Malta, standing in the airport lounge with a suitcase under each arm having already been warned by Alex Sears not to come back.' He put his hands up to seven major robberies with Chopper Knight and the rest of the team, including the previously mentioned Blackwall Tunnel robbery. We never recovered any of his money. Ellen Whale, his wife, insisted the money for their expensive holiday in Malta came from previous robberies for which he had already served his time in prison.

Bernie Khan was the next robber to be targeted. On Friday, 15 September 1978, Ohio officers successfully kept surveillance on Patricia Sims, Khan's girlfriend, who was visiting her husband, Arthur Sims, in HM Prison Maidstone. She was followed to an address in Bethnal Green, London. As she was about to enter this address, Bernie Khan was seen to leave in a Volkswagen Passat with the registration SMD 333S.

As Khan drove off, he recognised two Kent officers who had arrested him in the past. He sped away, followed by the officers who called for assistance. He was eventually bottled up in Delta Street E2. At this stage two of our armed officers walked towards him, but he accelerated and drove the car directly at them. One of the officers fired three shots at him, which caused him to crash. He abandoned his car and made good his escape on foot into a large housing estate. Despite a most intensive search lasting several hours he was lost. All three bullets had penetrated the car, one shattering the windscreen, but it had to be chalked up as another show of bad police marksmanship!

On 6 October 1978, we received good information that Chopper Knight, the leader of the team, was to keep a 'meet' in Solebay Street, off the Mile End Road, East London. Chopper was very much surveillance-conscious, and all our units were told to keep some distance from the area.

I remember Colin Kinnaird was the main eyeball. He was perched on top of a church spire with a pair of binoculars. He was the first to recognise Chopper and he gave all our other units directions as to what he was doing. Chopper got into a Fiat driven by Theresa Seagars, wife of John Seagars, our supergrass. The area was surrounded by some 40 officers, including a contingent from the robbery squad led by Detective Chief Inspector Dave Bassett.

The order was given to move in. Chopper noticed a posse of armed officers approaching from all sides of the car as a police vehicle blocked the road. He took over the wheel and made a desperate attempt to avoid capture, driving on the pavement and smashing into any vehicle in his path. He was driving like a lunatic with no regard for anyone. Police were just as desperate to arrest him. Dave Bassett managed to get his hand on the driver's door, and the windscreen was eventually smashed. Suffice to say he was eventually overpowered, arrested and handcuffed. Theresa Seagars was not injured, apart from a couple of small cuts and splinters of glass in her clothing.

We were quite amazed that Chopper was not armed. He had £500 on him when he was arrested. He was another likeable rogue, a professional who I enjoyed interviewing. Far more so than the up-and-coming drug-dealing shits we have nowadays.

Chopper would not sign any confession but talked freely about his involvement. He admitted he was the organiser of the team, the one who found the work, allocated each individual their jobs on robberies, made the decisions to split-second timing, stole and plated the cars used for the robberies and distributed the robbery shares as well as expenses for the bent security guards for information they supplied. After every crime Chopper collected all the weapons, keeping them in his possession until the next robbery, with the exception of Jim Moody's (he kept his own two sawn-off shotguns). None of his monies from any of his robberies was ever recovered. We estimated he had a personal share of £400,000 – a lot of money in 1978.

During the late 70s and 80s all armed robbers were advised by (dodgy) legal representatives to make allegations that they were beaten up in custody. This was always the claim, especially if any of them made admissions to their guilt. We were well aware of this advice. When Chopper was in custody at Epsom Police Station I handcuffed him and took him out to the station yard on the pretext I was exercising him. We arranged for a photographer to attend and he took a splendid shot of Chopper and me joking away. Chopper was in great form.

There was a gypsy horse and cart in the yard and I suggested to Chopper it would make a good getaway vehicle. I continued to joke with him and kept him laughing. Epsom Police Station is in the flight path of London Airport and a jumbo jet passed overhead when we were in the yard. I said to Chopper, 'There's a Concorde, Charlie.' Chopper replied, 'If it is, it's a Scottish Concorde, Jock, because the plane we are looking at is a jumbo jet.' Sure enough, when the case came to trial allegations of assault were made against us. However, when the photos of Chopper and me were produced any such allegations were soon dropped.

Chopper was extremely careful with his money. After the Banstead Robbery the team met in Jim Moody's flat over in East London. Chopper counted out each individual share, which came to £96,000. As John Seagars was about to leave the flat with his share, Chopper stopped him and asked for the £100 he owed him. Seagars had to pay him there and then, otherwise he would not have left the flat in good health.

Sammy Benefield (known within the team as 'the Scotsman') came from Peterhead, the same town as Bill Forman, our Detective Inspector. As mentioned before, Benefield was one of our supergrasses. Chopper was not impressed when I started humming my favourite song, 'I've just come down from the Isle of Skye...'

'Shut up Jock!' he shouted, 'There's enough singing Scotsmen on this team!'

Alex Sears was arrested in the Telegraph public house in Stratford, East London, by two Essex officers, Colin Atkins and Roy Clarke. He had been dropped off by his current girlfriend, Vivian Minchington. Vivian was the wife of Johnny the Bosh, a well-known safebreaker who was in prison doing 22 years for robbing the Bank of America of millions of pounds.

Sears was taken to Greenwich Police Station after his arrest. His verbal statement to Bill Forman was, 'You know we have done the robberies of which I am accused – I know I have done the robberies I have been accused of – but proving them is a different matter.'

Detective Inspector Ernie Brown of Tayside Police formally charged Sears with an armed robbery in Dundee. Sears pleaded not to be sent across the border to Scotland as he feared he would disappear forever.

When the officers entered the charge, Sammy Benefield, our supergrass, happened to be there at the same time. Sears made a heroic attempt to attack Benefield and was restrained, but he vowed he or other members of the team would get him.

Prior to Jim Moody's arrest we had had numerous sightings of him and searched many, many addresses. One particular Saturday an informant rang me to say Jim Moody was in a caravan in Naze Down on the Isle of Sheppey. I rang Bill Forman, who asked me to accompany him to Naze Down. On the way we picked up Maggie Grimble, a WPC who was seconded to our squad.

We met the informant and the information he gave us was, to say the least, a bit vague. Suffice it to say we found no trace of Jim Moody. We had a few drinks in a local club and were making our way home when we had another call from the informant via Scotland Yard, that he had housed (located) Big Jim Moody.

We did a U-turn and back we went to Naze Down. We met the informant, who told us Moody was in a certain pub on the island and even pointed out the pub to us. This was at about 9 pm. I hid in a ditch, keeping an eye on the pub, while Bill and Maggie went to arrange for the armed Kent Task Force to come to our assistance. I was frozen lying in that ditch, and to my annoyance the publican decided to have a 'lock-in'. The first customers to leave went at 2 am, and I informed Bill over the radio that there was movement.

We followed punters to a caravan further down the road which was then surrounded by armed police. Arc lights were set up which lit the caravan site. Bill had a loudspeaker and used it to say, 'Jim, come out with your hands in the air.' A few seconds went by, then the occupant opened the door, shouted 'Fuck off!' and went back inside.

Bill got on the loudhailer again and shouted, 'Armed police – come out with your hands up.' The fellow opened the door and said, 'What the fuck's happening?' Bill shouted to me, 'Handcuff him. Jock,' which I did. I immediately realised he was nothing like Jim Moody. 'Oh shit!' I thought.

Bill soon thought the same. I asked him for the handcuff keys to unlock the prisoner from me, but he didn't have any keys to fit them. Kent handcuffs were different to those used by the Met. Bill then had a brainstorm. He got on to the nearest Met Police Station to the Kent border, which I think was St Mary Cray. He asked the station officer there to send a car down with a set of keys, but once again was promptly told to fuck off. I had to sit in the charge room of Naze Down Police Station handcuffed to this innocent guy for at least two hours. Fortunately he had a sense of humour and he actually enjoyed the chat I had with him.

Eventually Bill Forman decided to call the local Fire Brigade, who cut the handcuffs and freed us. We apologised profusely to the man, who was an East End of London car dealer. He didn't complain; the only thing he wanted was the bits and pieces of the handcuffs as a souvenir, but we could not give him these as we thought there would be a big enquiry. However, that was the last we heard of it.

A few months later our informant answered a knock at his door and was shot dead.

All the men who had been arrested were charged with three robberies: the Banstead robbery, a robbery in the Blackwall Tunnel and a robbery at Rochester Post Office.

The two supergrasses, Benefield and Seagars, were sentenced to five years each and had 41 other offences taken into consideration. These two men were abused by the rest of the team when they were giving evidence against them. Supergrasses are a necessary evil in the fight against armed robbers, or for that matter any serious offence. I don't think any of the Ohio officers admired the supergrasses, but their evidence was necessary. All of the accused were convicted and sentenced to a total of 218 years.

Chopper Knight got 18 years. Before sentencing, Judge Justice Stoker said to Chopper, 'I have not the slightest doubt that you were the leader and a very good one too. You would have been the leader in any field you choose to follow. You chose this one. You are a very dangerous man. These robberies of which you have been convicted showed a high degree of organisation and extremely careful planning and execution.' Later the Judge told the team as a whole, 'You all possess qualities which would have fitted you as leaders among your fellow men. You are extremely intelligent with abilities of organisation and planning and you all possess courage. It's tragic that you used these qualities to make war on us.'

The trials were heard at Maidstone Crown Court and lasted for three months. Just before they got under way we had information that there was a £100,000 contract out in the underworld to have our supergrasses killed. Senior officers took this threat seriously, and security was increased at the court and in the surrounding streets and buildings. We, as members of Ohio, transferred the prisoners in armour-plated police vans with further police armed escorts from the prison to Maidstone Crown Court. They were considered too dangerous for the Prison Service to do the escort. Witnesses had armed escorts. We strongly suspected Jim Moody, who was still at large, was behind this threat.

On Friday, 21 December 1979, an Irishman called John Kennedy was stopped by Customs and Excise at Gatwick Airport on his arrival in the UK from Dallas, Texas. He was in possession of a box of chocolates in which two .38 revolvers were concealed, together with 100 rounds of ammunition. At the time the IRA was creating havoc on mainland Britain, but Kennedy did not want to be associated with the IRA or labelled as a terrorist. He asked if he could speak to officers from Operation Ohio. Bill Forman and Det. Sgt. Jim Davies went to the airport to see him.

Kennedy told the officers that Jim Moody was renting his flat at 186 Coldharbour Lane, Brixton, while he was over in America. He further stated that the guns and the ammunition were for Moody. Kennedy drew a plan of the inside of his flat and furnished the officers with the telephone number.

At 5 am on Saturday 22 December, armed Ohio officers led by Charlie Snape surrounded the flat in Brixton. We were assisted by D11 officers, who are the appointed firearms officers for the Met. The whole operation was geared up for a possible siege, with the surrounding streets closed to traffic and pedestrians diverted.

Bill Forman asked another officer to read out the telephone number Kennedy had given us for the flat. When Bill dialled the number it was answered by a lady. Bill told her to put Jim Moody on the line. The woman didn't have a clue what Bill was on about and told him so in no uncertain terms. Bill came off the phone and told us he had just been speaking to Lady Beaverbrook, who actually lived in Mayfair. She was not happy to be disturbed at 5 am! Although we were all keyed up waiting for the elusive Jim, we had a good laugh at Bill's expense. But Bill was under pressure and did not appreciate us taking the piss.

He then dialled the right number, which was answered by Jim Moody. When Jim looked out of the window and saw the amount of weapons pointing at him, he realised his time was up.

Bill had a conversation with Moody and told him to not to try to do a runner or play any silly games. Moody then said, 'What about my boy?' This was the first time we were aware that his son Jason was with him. That put a spanner in the works. Jim asked for ten minutes to get them both ready and Bill agreed. During the ten minutes' grace he was given Moody started stuffing £20, £10 and £5 notes down the toilet in an effort to get rid of incriminating evidence. Eventually the toilet got blocked. Bill got on the phone again and told him to send Jason out with his hands up. I have to say we all felt sorry when little Jason came out. He was just a kid and it must have been pretty traumatic for him.

We gathered all the banknotes we recovered from the toilet together, and they came to £910. When Moody was questioned later he said he thought he had flushed £40,000 down the drain.

The rest of his robbery team, apart from Bernie Khan, had been put on trial, found guilty and sentenced. Jim Davies and Ray Sutherland searched the flat and found all the statements relating to the robberies the others had been convicted of. Moody was well aware of the evidence against him before his arrest. He was taken to Brixton Police Station where he was interviewed at length by Mr Forman and Mr Snape, before being charged like the others with three armed robberies, the Blackwall Tunnel, the Banstead robbery and Rochester Post Office.

Jim Moody was fond of his mother Rosina, whom I knew as I had searched her flat on numerous occasions. She was run over in a hit-and-run accident in Rosendale Road, Dulwich, and died a short time before his arrest. He could not attend the funeral as he was on the run and knew that had he attended we would be there waiting for him.

I was handcuffed to Moody when we escorted him to court after he was charged. He asked us (there were five of us on the escort) if he could visit his mother's grave. We agreed to stop at West Norwood Cemetery. It was a bitterly cold morning with snow on the ground. We did not have time to make enquires as to where his mother was buried. We were also concerned he would try to escape. Instead the five of us chipped in £5 each and bought some flowers, which Jim placed by the gate of the cemetery. He appreciated what we had done for him, but he still owes us a fiver each!

I was still handcuffed to Jim at Greenwich Court. I had grown my hair shoulder-length and the resulting mop of bright ginger hair certainly did not make me look like a detective. When the case was called I accompanied Jim, still handcuffed, into the dock. The magistrate looked up, saw the two of us, and asked, 'Which one is the prisoner?'

I pointed to Jim and said, 'He is, Your Worship.'

Jim immediately pointed to me and said, 'No I'm not – he is, sir.' There was laughter in court. Jim was remanded in custody to Brixton Prison. We shall talk more about Jim Moody later.

Brian McIntosh was employed by Security Express as a driver/custodian. Sometime in 1977, whilst he was wearing the company uniform, he took his car to a garage run by a man called Geoff Welch. Welch told McIntosh he could put him in touch with someone (Chopper) who could earn him some extra money.

Welch did the introduction to Chopper and Moody. They gave McIntosh £50 here and there to have a drink and pay his phone bill so that they could always contact him. They started pressing him for information about the movements of Security Express vehicles and the routes they took. He initially gave them false information but they soon sussed him out. They threatened him with violence, and it got to the point that he was a very frightened man.

The first bit of information he gave them concerned a Security Express van that carried in excess of £500,000, and which normally stopped in a car park near Cambridge. Chopper organised a raid on this vehicle at the car park. They drove a furniture van alongside the security van, but the driver chucked the keys into some bushes and the attack was abandoned.

Chopper got back to McIntosh and told him to do a drawing of the inside of a Security Express van, and in particular of the area where the safe was located. He did this and handed it to Chopper. The team were able to do the Banstead robbery using this drawing. It was later recovered under the carpet at a flat at 29 Ben Jonson Road, E3, which was used as a safe house after several robberies. McIntosh had been paid £2,000 for this. He was arrested and charged, and he gave evidence against the robbers.

Brian Upton was another security guard, employed by Group 4. Chopper pressed Upton for information, and he supplied the gang with the route the security van took, as well as times and places of deliveries. This enabled the team to carry out the Blackwall Tunnel robbery. In return Upton was given a percentage of the cash (£3000) from the robbery. He pleaded guilty and gave evidence against the robbers, before being was sentenced to two and a half years in prison.

Vivian Minchington was the wife of Johnny the Bosh, a renowned safebreaker who was serving 22 years for the Bank of America robbery. While he was inside she was shacking up with Alex Sears. She was the most surveillance-conscious of anyone I ever knew. It was a nightmare trying to follow her. We had to at least double up our team to keep up with her.

After the team were arrested and remanded in Brixton, we received information that some members of the team had a prison officer in their pocket. We followed the prison officer and clocked him having a meet with Vivian. It was a lot easier to follow the prison officer than to follow Vivian. We covered another couple of meets and eventually captured them with tools to assist in an escape. Both were arrested.

The two supergrasses (or resident informers as they are now called), Benefield and Seagars, and the security guard Brian Upton who gave evidence for the prosecution, had to be exercised every day. We had to do this over and above our normal day's work. They lived in a cell in a police station and were supplied with more or less anything they wanted. We had no guidelines in these days as to what to do with them.

One day we were working very late and decided to have a few 'afters' in the pub next door to the nick. I remembered that Brian Upton had not been given his daily exercise, so I went back to the nick for him. I took him into the pub with me and had a few drinks. We left at about two in the morning. As we were walking towards the nick we heard a shout: 'Jock! Jock! You left me behind!' Upton had gone to the toilet and I had left him in the pub. The only exercise he got that day was running after me. Had he decided to escape I would have definitely been sacked

During the period I was looking after these supergrasses I was building a double garage at my house. The foundations had to be dug, lorry-loads of blocks and cement bags unloaded, shingle mixed by hand and timber cut to size. The supergrasses came in extremely handy, and the garage was built pretty quick and pretty cheap. They were so good that all my neighbours wanted the name of the building company I was using.

The trial was at Maidstone Crown Court and lasted for three months. Several of the accused refused to go into the witness box. Chopper Knight read a prepared statement consisting of 58 pages from the witness box. In this he gave most of the officers who interviewed him a mention. He had about six pages which featured me and Mick Flack, who was a DS on the squad.

In referring to me, Chopper said, 'I will ask you to take a close look at DC Murray. Is he the clown he makes out to be, or is he a very shrewd police officer? He did admit to having a big stick on the morning of my arrest. And a pickaxe handle come to that. The one he said he got from his garage. And what about the photograph that we have seen from the dirty tricks department? That's a clever touch, to get me laughing at a joke, get a hidden camera to snap the occasion and then present the evidence if I complain of harassment or ill-treatment. And what about the joke he said made us both laugh. He says, looking up in the sky, "There's a Concorde, Charlie," and I reply, "If it is, that's a Scottish Concorde, because the plane we are looking at is a jumbo jet." And he stood in that witness box and said he still doesn't see what the joke is. Everyone else did. Anyway, we were not laughing about a Scottish Concorde at all. As we came out of Epsom Police Station we came out into a very large car park, and among the vehicles parked there, there was a four-wheeled cart with the shafts up in the air, and all old iron in the back. And we laughed when Murray said to me, 'That would make a good getaway car.' Treat Mad Jock Murray's evidence with extreme caution, members of the Jury. He's not as mad as he makes out.'

Jim Moody's Escape

Although we had put Jim Moody into Brixton Prison he was such a powerful man in the underworld that our boss Mr Snape always feared there would be an attempt to free him. He warned the prison authorities accordingly, and they assured him no one ever escaped from the wing of the prison where he was, D-Wing. Moody was classed as A category. Among the inmates with him were the most feared criminals in the land, including Gerard Tuite, the famous IRA bomber. Moody, Tuite and a fellow robber, Stan Thompson, were all on the same floor in D-Wing. Moody arranged through his wife and brother for tools to be smuggled in to assist them in escaping. All three removed bricks from their adjoining cell walls and made holes large enough for them to crawl through to the cell occupied by Tuite. Tuite's cell was on the outside wall, which would eventually be their route to freedom.

On Monday 15 December 1980, they made their final breakthrough. They made dummies out of newspapers and clothing, which they put under their blankets, and got out onto the roof. Avoiding the CCTV camera, they made their way to the outside wall, climbed over it and into the outside world. They stopped a passing minicab which took them to the Herne Hill area of south London.

Jim Moody avoided capture for 13 years, until he was finally shot dead in the Royal public house in Victoria Park, Hackney. During part of the time he was on the run he lived in a flat in Kennington, where I was stationed during the period. Had I come across him I would never, ever have tried to arrest him on my own. I had already felt the muscles on his body when I was handcuffed to him to take him to court. I can say without question he scared me. He was an animal who police suspected of many murders.

12

Tower Bridge 1980–1982

During 1979 I was serving on the Regional Crime Squad. There was a spate of burglaries reported in South London and Sussex in which safes were attacked using gas cutting equipment. Safe-breaking using oxy-acetylene was a thing of the past. I received information that a man called Brian Richardson was responsible for these crimes, and when I checked up on him he did have convictions for similar offences.

I mounted an operation on him. He was a most difficult, almost impossible, target to follow. He also was as bold as brass. One night he came up to the driver of our black cab which was tailing him and said, 'You're from the blue light club in Victoria Street.' Cheeky bastard!

I noticed he took the same route from his home address in Sutton to Crawley in Sussex every evening. As his route was known, it was decided just to man the traffic junctions he went through rather than follow him. We were successful using this method and eventually found out who his partner in crime was, a man named Peter Field.

As most of the burglaries were committed in Sussex, we called in No 6 Regional Crime Squad, who were responsible for the Sussex area. A joint operation we called 'Operation Villiers' was formed. After several weeks he was eventually captured on a job with all the oxy-acetylene equipment. On 18 April he appeared at Lewes Crown Court, together with Field. They admitted a further 33 offences and were sentenced to a total of 5 years. Both No 9 and No 6 Regional Crime Squad officers were commended by the Judge.

I returned to Division in 1980, having spent six eventful years at the Yard. The chain of command for Divisional CID had changed over the years I was serving at the Yard. Senior uniform officers up to Commander were now in charge of the CID. Operation Countryman was still investigating corruption in the Met CID, and I was interviewed by them twice for allegations made against me by serving prisoners. These were proved to be malicious and without foundation.

Rotherhithe and Bermondsey are a breeding ground for armed robbers. When I was on squads attached to the Yard I had spent most of my time sitting and waiting outside pubs and clubs and following suspects. I now expected to reverse my role and frequent these pubs to feed squads at the Yard with information about robbers, their associates and places they frequented.

There is one thing that happens to all successful officers – jealousy from other officers creeps in. Allegations start to circulate that the busy officer is either bent, corrupt or a liar. There are many, many good officers whose careers have been ruined through unsubstantiated allegations, some of them coming from jealous colleagues.

During this period the uniform senior officers frowned on any of the CID who frequented pubs. I came in from the pub one lunchtime and called in at the reserve room, where I met for the first time our uniform Superintendent.

He asked, 'Are you Jock?'

'Yes sir,' I replied.

He said, 'I've heard about you. How come you know all the villains on this patch?'

'How come you know that I know all the villains on this patch?' was my response.

'I just heard,' he said.

'No, that's not the reason, Guv,' I answered. 'You think I know all these villains because you think I am corrupt. You think I am a bent copper.'

He made no reply and left the room.

Morale was at a low ebb in the CID. I noticed this as soon as I entered the office at Tower Bridge. None of the officers wanted to work – they were scared of their own shadows. There was plenty of crime on M Division, more than any other division in London, I suspect. Every second week we had a murder and our patch was over-run with top-class robbers like John 'Little Legs' Lloyd, Billy Tobin, the Arif brothers, Kenny Noye, John Flemming and many others. Senior uniform officers didn't give a toss, and certainly did not encourage CID to get stuck in. As far as they were concerned they were quite happy to drift – their motto was 'don't rock the boat'.

I continued to work as I always did, frequenting pubs, cultivating informants, making as many arrests as possible, passing information to squads at the Yard. No one ever said anything to me after the day I confronted my uniform Superintendant, and I know now that this officer actually supported me afterwards. I was very successful at Tower Bridge.

I had information that a man, Frederick Bailey, living on an estate on Rotherhithe's patch, was in possession of a handgun and that he was currently engaged in robberies. I made discreet enquiries and traced him to an address on a council estate in Rotherhithe where it was impossible to keep observation from a vehicle. I did eventually find a suitable, if freezing, place in an abandoned warehouse. It was a cold, cold winter, the water pipes had burst, and there were several inches of ice on the floor. The suspect was only in my view as he came down a set of three steps, then he passed out of my sight.

I bypassed all ranks and went direct to the uniform Commander in charge of the Division. I told him the information I had and what I had achieved by way of evidence so far on my own. He was a good senior officer. He asked why I had jumped five ranks and come straight to him. I told him that I didn't think my immediate senior officers would show any interest in the surveillance or deal with it in the way I wanted, and this satisfied him.

CID officers had a diary which had to be completed daily,

giving all their movements during working hours. This was in turn inspected and countersigned by the DI. The Commander told me that when I filled in my diary I should put in, 'Working directly for the Commander'.

The DI was not at all happy that I refused to tell him what I was doing, but the Commander fully trusted me, knowing I had plenty of experience from my postings at the Yard. Eventually I identified a vehicle used by Bailey. I now believed I had enough information to ask C11 (Special Surveillance Squad at the Yard) for assistance.

As a direct result of my information, 'Operation Rabbit' was formed by C11 officers – they had access to many facilities to assist in this type of work. My Commander authorised me to be seconded to C11 for the duration of this operation.

At the time, September 1981, there were a series of rather disturbing offences of robbery and burglary artifice (the legal term for obtaining entry to a premises by deception for the purposes of theft). A gang of ruthless men, posing as police officers, sometimes wearing uniform, would gain entry to houses by producing false warrant cards and search warrants. Occasionally, when their ruse failed to get them in, they resorted to violence by the production of guns to threaten the householder. We suspected that Bailey and his associates were the team responsible. Deputy Assistant Commissioner David Powis was so concerned that he was about to form a special squad to deal with them.

Their disguises were very convincing. In one particular case they entered a house posing as police officers with search warrants and, having searched it for stolen goods, took property away stating they would return it if it was not identified as stolen. When the property was not returned the victim complained, and the matter was investigated by officers from the Complaints Department at the Yard.

Details of all similar offences, both in the Metropolitan Police District and surrounding Force areas, were collated and analysed. Numerous enquiries were carried out regarding Bailey's associates, descriptions were co-ordinated and a vast amount of surveillance work was carried out. Suffice to say we identified all the team.

These were professional, cunning criminals who took anti-surveillance measures to escape being followed by the police. In January, 1982, after many weeks of frustrating enquiries and after consultation with other members of the Squad, it was decided to arrest the four suspects and place them on identification parades in connection with the offences for which we considered them responsible.

On 25 January 1982, a series of identification parades took place at Barnet Police Station. These lasted for four days, and 25 witnesses were brought from all over London and surrounding Police Force areas in an effort to get them identified for offences. Subsequently further identification parades were held at Kennington Police Station for two days, and again over ten witnesses attended. This led to the four men being picked out by six different witnesses for three different offences and they were charged. They vehemently denied all charges.

After a five-week trial in which police evidence was attacked strongly and the jury were out for two days and a night, all four were convicted. Three were sentenced to four years' imprisonment. The fourth, a man by the name of Whitlock, who had been on bail, failed to appear at court on the day the jury were sent out to consider their verdict. On this day, in the early hours of the morning, he had received severe injuries to his leg from 30 pellets from a shotgun, fired at him at close range outside his home.

Detective Sergeant Bernie Page, the officer from the Regional Crime Squad involved in the paperwork for the case, interviewed Whitlock several times. Whitlock eventually confessed that the wound was self-inflicted to gain the sympathy of the jury. In addition, he admitted many further offences of dishonestly handling stolen property. I was delighted with the result, which had started off with my information, then involved assistance by C11 and arrests by C12 (Regional Crime Squad) – a typical example of a divisional and inter-squad operation.

Hiding from the Law

A 16-year-old with the family name Taylor was heavily involved in burglary of household properties and business premises alike. We knew his identity and where he lived, but he evaded all attempts to capture him. He entered premises through the smallest gap, window or air vent. He had been identified by fingerprint evidence at several break-ins, so once he was caught there would be no problem charging him.

One morning at 4 am the telephone rang at my home. It was the Station Officer from Tower Bridge, to tell me that one of my informants was at the counter and wanted to speak to me urgently. I told him to let him speak to me and he did. The informant simply said, 'He is home now.' I knew straight away whom he was referring to and I was in the station by 4.40 am. The informant was quite confident that Taylor was at home and I arranged for the flat to be searched. I had searched it several times before, so I was aware of its layout.

Taylor's sister was the only person indoors. She was a rather big lady – I don't really mean lady – about 18 stone, wearing a long nightdress. She stood in the middle of the living room cursing and swearing at me. At one stage I remember her shouting, 'Jock Murray, I wouldn't piss on your grave!'

We eventually gave up the search and left. I went back to my car where the informant was waiting. I gave him a mouthful for calling me out at that time of the morning. He was adamant Taylor was still inside. All of a sudden it dawned on me that there was only one place he could be hiding. I went back indoors and said to his sister, 'If you do have a piss now you might drown your brother instead of me. Come out, you little bastard!' Out peeps little Taylor from under her nightdress.

Arrest of a Compulsive Liar

I was on early turn one morning dealing with prisoners held overnight. Normal procedure in all CID offices is for the night-duty staff to leave a record of what happened during their tour of duty. In this case, an entry read, 'There is one in the cells for Going Equipped [to commit an offence] but he won't have the time of day, he refuses to answer any questions, be careful when dealing with him. This man is an inveterate liar, must be treated with caution.'

I spent the morning questioning him. I told him what the other officers who had dealt with him in the past thought of him, and not to expect any favours from me. I leaned on him pretty heavily. I told him the offence he was arrested for was petty, and could be over and done with the same day.

For some reason his attitude changed. Perhaps I dealt with him differently from the way he had been treated in the past. He went quiet for a while, then all of a sudden he came out with, 'You impress me, Jock. Can you make enquiries and see if there has been a murder on the other side of the river not far from Cable Street?' I asked him why I should do this, and when he told me he might be able to help, I ridiculed him and told him not to play silly buggers with me. However, he eventually convinced me he might have something to tell.

I made enquiries at Leman Street Police Station, and they confirmed a murder was currently being investigated. The Officer Manager gave me a brief outline of what had happened. I went back to the cells and told the prisoner there had been a murder. He just said, 'I told you so.'

I had a gut feeling he knew more, and when I questioned him further, he told me the murder involved a group of Road Rats (a motorbike gang similar to the Hell's Angels) and he knew the house where the murder took place. I handcuffed him, and together with another officer took him across the river where he pointed out the suspect house. We then returned to Tower Bridge Police Station.

The murder squad officers at Leman Street confirmed we had the correct house. The premises had already been forensically examined but they had found nothing. The prisoner insisted the body had been cut up in that house. He went further, and said, 'I can show you where the head and hands are hidden.' Officers on the murder squad had the house examined again for forensic evidence, and this time the results were positive. I handed the prisoner to the murder squad officers, arrests were made and the murder was solved. I never heard anything by the way of a thank-you from that murder squad.

Murder Enquiries

When Detective Chief Superintendent Graham Melvin took command of M Division CID, he was a breath of fresh air. He was an old-style copper who led by example, and he backed the troops. Everyone wanted to work for him and morale improved noticeably.

Graham had his hands full with murders. I think he had at least four running at the same time. A lot of them were to do with drugs and drug dealers shooting each other.

I was involved in all the murders in one way or the other. In fact Mr Melvin appointed Malcolm Goldie and me as liaison officers for all the murders running in South East London at the time. One particular murder was that of Paddy O'Nion from the Bermondsey area. The main suspect was traced to Coventry where he was arrested. He was a bad, bad man. When the Met officers went to take him back to London, he ripped the heels from his shoes. He had a heel in each hand with the nails sticking out and threatened anyone who came near him. He had to be overpowered and unfortunately died in the struggle. This was the type of individual we had to deal with on a South East London murder.

One lunchtime we had a murder in Rotherhithe. The usual procedures were followed: house-to-house enquiries, a search for witnesses, forensic examination of the scene, checking for fingerprints and photography. By evening a murder room was operational from Southwark Police Station.

Mr Melvin arranged for Special Patrol Group to assist us. He also arranged for a 5 am briefing and everyone went home for a kip to be ready for the early start. The office was of course manned 24 hours, and an officer manager was appointed to monitor all calls coming in during the night.

In fact I didn't go home – I went to the Crystal Tavern pub on my own. This pub was close to the murder scene and was next door to a car front owned by the notorious Charlie Wilson of the Great Train Robbery (he was murdered in 1990). The pub was used mostly by Charlie's henchmen, and was not a place frequented by police. I had sat outside it many times, waiting, watching and following criminals when I was serving on squads at Scotland Yard.

Towards closing time I went to the toilet. Soon afterwards a man followed me in there. He said, 'I suppose you are on the murder squad.'

When I told him I was, he put a piece of paper in my hand and said, 'A young girl at that address will tell you who did the murder.' He then made an about-turn and quickly left the toilets.

The address he gave me was in Southend. I went back to the murder office and said I wanted to book out a CID car to drive to Southend. The night duty officer manager refused to give me the keys to a police car, claiming I was over the limit to drive (he was not a bad judge). I grabbed hold of a uniform PC from the night relief who drove me down to Southend. There I met a girl aged about 14 and her father. She told me she could point out a flat in one of three identical blocks where the murderer had gone after he killed his victim. Unfortunately she did not know the exact address.

By this time it was around 2 am. The father and the girl came up to London with us, and she showed us three blocks of 15-storey flats off the Old Kent Road. She told us the man who committed the murder went into one of those blocks and into the ground floor flat on the corner. One could not blame her for not remembering the exact flat, as all three blocks were identical.

I got a few uniform colleagues to give me a hand searching the premises (without search warrants). I crashed through the door of the first flat, only to find an old lady living on her own. A quick fruitless search was made, she accepted my apologies, and off we went to the next one. A bunch of flowers was sent to her the next morning.

I did the same with the next door with the same result. This time there was an old couple living together. I left a uniform officer with them to explain our actions, and this satisfied them. I then attacked the last door. This flat was occupied by half a dozen teenagers. I shouted, 'You are all nicked for murder!'

The teenager nearest to me said, 'I didn't do the murder, but I am over the side from prison.' They were all arrested. They told us the name of the man who had committed the murder and that he had shaved his hair off to disguise himself. They also named the club in Bayswater where we could find him.

These enquiries took me to 5 am. When Mr Melvin and the rest of the troops came in he organised a team to go to the night-club where the suspect was arrested. Mr Melvin was delighted, but sent me home insisting I had worked enough hours. I don't know if he had my overtime claims in mind! The rest of the troops were not so happy. They were expecting a few weeks of hard-worked overtime.

Around this time another enquiry started at Scotland Yard. It was to deal with victims of the infamous Charlie Richardson gangsters. These were witnesses who had been tortured by Richardson and his team, but were too scared to give evidence against them at the trial. This enquiry was led by Commander Len Gillet, with a Detective Chief Superintendent in operational charge. I was seconded to this squad.

All the allegations were from years back and it was difficult to get corroborating evidence. We eventually arrested several people. I used to pick up the Chief Superintendent every morning and take him home at night. This was the first time I had worked for him. As the suspects were arrested he insisted, for some reason, that I interview them with him. Eventually the case was listed for trial at the Old Bailey, and a couple of days beforehand the Chief Superintendent tried to commit suicide by cutting his wrists. I have no idea why he wanted to do such a terrible thing, but it ended his days in the police. The trial went ahead but without the evidence of my senior officer. The suspects were all acquitted.

Georgie Francis and George Plummer

I knew Georgie Francis and George Plummer as criminals of the highest degree from my days on the squad. They both had business premises on Rotherhithe's patch. Francis was a likeable rogue who had a transport and freight company as a front. He shared his yard with another formidable criminal, George Plummer (not his real name), who was an importer of Parmesan cheese. When I was on the squad I targeted them from time to time, but never had enough definite information to set up an operation on them.

I was in the office one day when a colleague answered the telephone. He said, 'It's for you, Jock.' I asked who it was and he told me that the caller refused to say, that he only wanted to speak to me. It was George Plummer. He wanted to see me at his warehouse urgently.

Now George had many convictions, including one, I believe, for murder or attempted murder of his father-in-law. This had happened one day when George was at home and there was loud knocking on his door. George thought it was another team of criminals after him. He fired his shotgun through the door, and when he opened it, he found he had shot his father-in-law.

When I got to his warehouse he was pacing up and down and cursing everything in sight. He told me he had had a container-load of skateboards stored in Georgie Francis's yard, and it had disappeared while they were having their lunch. Skateboards had just come out and were all the rage at the time.

I thought, 'Oh yeah, this has got to be an insurance job,' but as it happened the load was not insured. I asked why he had specified me as I had never met him before. He just said, 'I've heard of you – you have a reputation.'

I went and spoke to Georgie Francis, who denied any involvement. I did the usual forensic examination and told Plummer I would be in touch. 'Jock,' he said, 'find out who the bastards are and there's a good drink in it for you.'

I returned to the station and made a few phone calls. I circulated a description of the container and the stolen skateboards via the property index. At the same time, I thought, 'Here are two top-class villains reporting a theft to me.' I was a bit suspicious about the situation and gave it a little thought.

There was one bad man I didn't particularly like that I could never nail down to any crime, although I knew he was 'well at it'. I met with Plummer again and told him I had a whisper that so-and-so had nicked the skateboards. He replied, 'Fuck me, I never thought of him, Jock! You could be right – leave it to me.'

A week or so later, I had a call from Plummer who asked me to meet him again. When I did I hardly recognised him. He had two beautiful black eyes and a big grin all over his face. 'Yes Jock, you were right. Leave the rest to me.'

He did not want me to continue investigating the crime, so it was written up and classified as 'No Crime'. I have no idea what happened, or if George recovered his skateboards.

I got to know Georgie Francis through his daughter, who had been sexually assaulted. I went to see her at her parents' address in Knockholt. It was a large country house worth a lot of money. Georgie was a little bit of a showman, and that day he was in top form. After I took a statement from his daughter he came in with a whole side of sirloin steak and asked how thick I would like my steak – half an inch, an inch, an inch and a half? I think he ended up at about 2 inches of steak, which he served with spaghetti bolognaise and a bottle of red wine. A couple of weeks later he was nicked for stealing a lorry-load of washing machines and a short time after that he was murdered.

Break-in at a Cash and Carry

By far the worst job I ever had to deal with when I was stationed at Tower Bridge was a break-in at Tarry's Cash and Carry, just off the Old Kent Road. It was broken into overnight, and as the early-turn CID officer it was down to me to investigate. When I arrived at the scene it was a total shambles. Entry had been gained through the roof, and a large quantity of wines, beers and spirits had been taken. One could see at a glance it was not the work of professionals. A van belonging to the company had also been stolen and driven through the shop doors. It had obviously been loaded with the stolen booze beforehand. This in a nutshell was what I had to investigate, quite a straightforward job on the face of it. After the usual initial enquiries I returned to the station.

Now, it so happens that the boundary between the patches of Tower Bridge Police Station and Peckham Police Station is the Old Kent Road. A couple of hours later Peckham CID telephoned to say that twelve Irish tramps had been found absolutely legless in derelict houses on the Peckham side of the Old Kent Road. The Tarry's Cash and Carry van was also there with the doors wide open, still half-full of booze. All the buggers had been arrested and taken to Peckham.

Peckham CID asked if we'd had a burglary at Tarry's. In view of what they had told me about the arrest of the tramps, my initial reaction was to deny any knowledge. But as I knew full well that within a few minutes they would find out, there was no point in keeping up a pretence.

I went over to Peckham where I met a relieved DC with a big smile on his face. All he said was, 'Be my guest, Jock. You can take over now.' I was confronted in the detention room with the filthiest scene I ever saw. There were bodies everywhere, lying in human excreta, vomit and piss. The stench was incredible. Before any of them could be interviewed they had first to be hosed down and given a change of clothing.

I thought long and hard about an easy way out of the appalling situation. I tried to make a deal with the tramps, offering to charge one of them and let the rest go. No way would they agree to this, mainly because they had free accommodation and food for as long as they were in custody. I ended up interviewing and charging all twelve. It was quite a scene at court the following morning as they all trooped into the dock.

Other officers attending with their own cases really took the mickey out of me. 'Jock, you're a real crime buster! Jock, can we join your squad?' It was 'Jock this' and 'Jock that'. The twelve all pleaded not guilty and elected to go for trial. The legal aid report to our solicitors was the longest report I had ever prepared. Their previous convictions alone came to 105 pages, but still the job had to be done. On top of that, when it came to trial they still pleaded not guilty. Basically, I was the only witness. When they were all found guilty, the learned magistrate at Tower Bridge Court decided they had spent long enough in custody and they were all released. It cost the taxpayer thousands. What a job!

John Bindon and His Friends

John Bindon was a criminal, an actor, a bully and a friend of Princess Margaret. I tried my best to cultivate him as an informant, but without success. During the late 60s there was an affray in the Ranleigh Club in Putney in which John Bindon was stabbed and nearly died. An associate of his dragged him out of the club before the police arrived and took him across the sea to Ireland. Bindon was known for the size of his willy. His party piece in the middle of a busy pub was to take out his prick and hang six half-pint glasses on it.

One Friday morning we were out early searching addresses. By 2 pm we had processed our prisoners and were heading home. We arranged to meet in the Worlds End pub for a drink before knocking off for the day. The pubs closed at 3 o'clock in those days. The bar was empty apart from four of us from the squad and a team of 'heavies' from West London.

It was obvious the publican was shit-scared of this team and they had him in their pocket. He was equally shit-scared of us, because if he continued serving we could take his licence off him. The situation began to get to a serious stage. The villains were 'fronting' us and no way were we going to move. In the end they gave up and walked out, but they were not happy with losing face. We got up to leave shortly afterwards.

One of our DCs went to the toilet as we headed for our individual cars. We happened to look back and saw the DC lying flat on his back in the gutter. John Bindon was standing over him. His mates who were in the pub had telephoned him to give them a hand but, of course, they had left the pub before he arrived. Bindon didn't know who our DC was and there was no sign of the rest of his team. Our man had been attacked from behind, but luckily he sustained no serious injury. The following morning when we raided the apartment of a society girl we found the team there. I can say we got our own back.

One of my watering holes in Knightsbridge was the Turk's Head. I used to drink there with a business friend. He introduced me to Johnny Bindon originally, and to the actor Richard Harris, his brother Dermot, John Murphy and a few other hardened drinkers.

On 3 November 1987, I met Richard Harris privately in the Halcyon Hotel, Holland Park Road. He told me he suspected that some of his family were using drugs. He believed the same supplier also supplied heroin to actors and actresses in the film industry. Richard wanted me to identify the supplier and he would deal with the person himself. He offered me a substantial fee if I could do this for him. I told him I was not a private detective and if I managed to identify the supplier I would arrest and prosecute him. I managed to do this without comprising him or his family.

John Murphy of the multi-millionaire civil engineering contractor family also told me of a dealer who he suspected was supplying his daughter with drugs. The same dealer was responsible for supplying drugs to many of the King's Road swinging 60s crowd. The arrest of both these dealers cleared up the supply of cocaine to high-society members in the Chelsea and Knightsbridge area of London. However, as soon as you put one dealer away another takes over, in a never-ending process. Richard Harris and John Murphy were something else, real hell-raisers. I often went with them to clubs and pubs where I met all sorts of people, including Christine Keeler. Christine was a regular in Paddy Kennedy's pub, the Star Tavern in Belgravia. I was accepted in this type of company, and as a result I gained a lot of information.

Abduction of a Child

On a weekend every station has a skeleton staff, unless of course there is serious work to hand that cannot be left until Monday. A senior officer of DI rank or above and a DS or DC would normally staff the office. This Sunday I was on with our Detective Chief Inspector. All was quiet, and he went home for the afternoon.

About 2.30 pm a call came over that a little girl who was playing in a park close to where her parents were having a drink had been abducted. She was last seen accompanied by a man going into a car. Fortunately someone took the number of the car, which I traced to an address. Meanwhile the driver had sussed he had been clocked and dropped off the girl unharmed. While abduction of a child is a serious crime, I didn't inform the DCI as I had everything in hand.

I arrested the driver and seized the vehicle. He would not answer any questions I put to him. His clothes and the girl's clothes were packaged for forensic examination. I took witness statements, the car was examined, everything was photographed. I believed I had enough circumstantial evidence to charge him, but decided to leave it until the result of the forensic examination. This man had numerous convictions for indecency with children and he had only been released from prison a few weeks earlier.

When the DCI came in after his Sunday dinner, I told him what had happened. He went potty: 'Why didn't you call me out?' I told him I had everything in hand and went through it stage by stage, and he agreed.

The result of the forensic examination was positive. Two fibres from the child's tracksuit were found on the suspect's clothing. I had ample evidence to convict, and he was charged accordingly.

He appeared at Inner London Crown Court, but when he was found not guilty I was gutted. The Lady Judge was also gutted, and she made her views known to the jury. She called me into her chambers and told me exactly what she thought. She then accompanied me to HMS *Belfast*, moored nearby, for refreshments.

The reason I tell this story is that I very nearly got sacked over it. The man involved was a minicab driver who used his own car, but the radio belonged to the taxi company. When the prisoner was released on bail, I restored the car to him but took the radio out before doing so. The radio was restored to the proprietor of the mini-cab firm.

He asked me the reason for the driver's arrest and I told him. I also told him he had numerous convictions for indecency with children. His reaction was, 'Fuck me! I get him to drive my children to school every morning.' He went after the driver and told him what I had said, called him all the dirty bastards under the sun and sacked him.

The driver made an official complaint against me and I was investigated by two senior officers. I denied all allegations against me, but this story shows the reader how careful one has to be.

Weekends on Duty

On another weekend I was on duty rota with the DCI. When I got to the office in the morning I read the night duty occurrence book. There was a prisoner in the cells to be interviewed. He would not answer any questions when the night duty CID officers interviewed him.

I took him out of the cells, introducing myself as Jock, and we went up to the CID office. I did the usual thing and offered him a cigarette. A prisoner is dying for a smoke after a night in the cells. When he sat down on a chair, I said, 'Are you expecting me to do the coffee? There's the kettle, the milk is in the little fridge. The boss wants a coffee, so go and clean three cups – two sugars in mine and one for the boss, and while the kettle is boiling, shall we have a chat about what you were up to last night.'

Another fag and he started singing like a bird. I took a statement under caution, and everything was done and dusted in half an hour.

I was pretty pleased with myself, so after he'd made the coffees and put them on a tray, I told him to follow me along the corridor to the Detective Chief Inspector's office.

I told him, 'When I knock on the door he will shout, "Come in". You walk in and just say, "Coffee, sir". When he asks, "Who the fuck are you?" just say, "I am a prisoner".'

The prisoner did as he was told. I was hiding behind the door, pissing myself laughing. As sure as God is in Glasgow these were the very words the DCI shouted when he saw him. He went further: 'And where is that bastard, Jock? Did he ask you to do this?'

He came storming out the door, and had I been a bit smaller I am sure he would have chinned me. I always worked well for that chief.

Auntie Kennag

My wife's auntie Kennag was a widow for at least 50 years. She was a lovely lady and lived until she was over 90. She stayed off Pentonville Road, next door to the prison in North London. If I was in the area to have a look at some premises or take a statement from someone, I used to take her with me just to pass the time for her.

When in the car, she got used to seeing me answering the radio, and this day I had left the radio on while I went into a house to take a statement. The radio was transmitting during my absence. When I got back to the car she had the mike in her hand and was shouting in Gaelic: '*Chan eil e an seo, chan eil e an seo!*' ('He's not here, he's not here!') They were not calling for me, but God knows what the switchboard operator at Scotland Yard would have thought had Kennag known how to press the transmitting button.

Kennag was a practising Christian, and all the ministers who came down from Scotland used to stay with her, along with their wives. I was up in North London this day and called in for a cup of tea. One of the minister's wives was also there. I could see her case was packed and she told me she was going to King's Cross Station to catch a train back to Scotland. I told her I would give her a lift when I finished my tea.

Auntie Kennag was in the kitchen. When I got up to go and said to the minister's wife, 'Give us your case', she ran into the kitchen shouting, 'I'm not going with that man!'

I wondered what the hell I had said to cause this. When she calmed down she explained to Kennag, 'He's just asked me to give him a kiss.'

On another occasion there was a minister and his wife in the house. They were going to catch some sort of public transport to Victoria. I offered them a lift which they gratefully accepted. On the way I thought I would give them a glimpse of Soho, just to see how they would react. I was driving down Shaftesbury Avenue when I saw a young PC being attacked by a couple of yobs. I stopped the car, jumped out, chinned them, sat on them and waited for police transport to arrive.

By this time traffic was at a standstill as my stationary car was blocking the road. Angry drivers surrounded my vehicle, and I think it was this day that the term 'road rage' was invented.

When I returned to the car the poor minister and his wife were petrified. I carried on as if nothing had happened. I bought them a coffee in Victoria Station, and all the man of the manse said was, 'That's the last time I'll accept a lift from you.'

13
On the Drugs Squad

When I was at Tower Bridge I arrested Ray Heather, who was a top-class villain. His father owned a jeweller's shop in Jamaica Road, Bermondsey. He was circulated as wanted in the *Police Gazette* by Lewisham Police for robbery. One day I was driving back to the station with my DI when I saw Heather driving his car, accompanied by a female passenger. We managed to stop the car and arrest him.

As I pulled him out he dropped a package containing drugs between the seats. He was charged accordingly, but when it came to trial his girl told the court the drugs belonged to her. In view of this, the charges against Heather for possession of drugs were withdrawn.

Two years later I was serving on the Central Drugs Squad attached to Scotland Yard. A very good informant of mine, Scotch Joe, told me that a man who he thought was a Swede was offering large amounts of cocaine for sale at £35,000 per kilo. Scotch Joe had met the target in J. Arthur's Club in Catford, South London, a club that was once owned by the infamous Richardson 'Torture Trial' family.

On 25 March 1986, I submitted a report to my then Detective Chief Superintendent, asking for permission for Scotch Joe to act as a 'participating informant', and he was duly allowed to arrange a meeting in the Clarendon Hotel, Blackheath, for me to negotiate a deal for the cocaine. Scotch Joe was to introduce me to the dealer.

Fortunately for me, and indeed for Scotch Joe, I decided to keep observation on the hotel until the target turned up, so I could then follow him into the hotel. When the target arrived, I immediately recognised him as Ray Heather, the person I had arrested two years earlier when I was serving at Tower Bridge. There was no way I could continue as a buyer.

John, one of our Detective Sergeants, volunteered at short notice to play my part. He did an excellent job, especially as he was not a recognised buyer on our team. Scotch Joe introduced John to Ray Heather and two other targets in the hotel as a drugs dealer from Edinburgh. They told John they could supply up to 10 kilos a week, but they would not deal with him unless he supplied them with an address and a telephone number in Edinburgh. A meeting was arranged for the following day.

An Edinburgh officer seconded to Scotland Yard Drugs Squad was able to supply us with an Edinburgh address and telephone number. This was actually checked out by the targets personally, and thankfully it satisfied them.

When John met them for the second time, he noticed one of the targets was armed. He told them he was not going to deal with them unless they were 'clean' (not armed). From then onwards everyone was searched for firearms, including the undercover officers. Heather stayed mostly in the background, using his mobile telephone and giving both the undercover officers and his flunkies instructions. On the final day of the operation we ended up in Battersea Park. Heather was in his Ferrari sports car. John gave our units a prearranged signal to say he had seen the drugs and it was time to arrest. Raymond John Heather, Patrick Francis Gallet and Kenneth Whitehead were duly arrested. This was a very satisfying job for me as I got my own back on Heather having me over two years earlier. They were all sentenced to long terms of imprisonment.

Scotch Joe was one of my best informants. On another occasion he was attacked and had a face wound that required 42 stitches. He was a divorced man who had custody of a two-year-old child whom he adored. On many an occasion I babysat her while he went out to work for me. In the end he became too well known, and I eventually managed to get him rehoused to a safe address in Cornwall. Through the information supplied by Scotch Joe I was able to liaise with Scottish police forces and have many of their targets arrested on their arrival at railway stations in Scotland, when carrying drugs supplied by London drug dealers.

One day I attended a drugs conference at the Yard. There were senior officers from various forces, including Scotland. I thought I recognised one of them, a Detective Superintendent from Glasgow. It was indeed Norman, one of my old schoolmates, whom I had not seen since the day we left school. I felt quite chuffed that here were the two of us from our humble background in the Outer Hebrides now targeting the most dangerous drug barons in Britain.

Richard Rowbotham was a major drug dealer who we had been following for a few weeks before I arrested him on 22 May 1976. We also had an OP (observation post) on his home address in Vernham Road, South London. My informant told me Rowbotham was expecting a delivery of a large quantity of cannabis, but he did not know exactly when. In such cases it's a matter of patience, waiting, watching and following. Information can come by other means and this can be at short notice.

This particular day two of us were in the OP when a transit van arrived at the address. Boxes were unloaded and taken indoors. It was a Friday afternoon and the rest of our team were busy on other jobs. We needed help and asked for assistance over the radio, but no one was available. Uniform lads from R District finally arrived, and we managed to arrest the whole team of five. They were all taken to Greenwich Police Station. The boxes contained 22 kilos of cannabis, valued at £70,000.

Later in the afternoon one of our DCs and a couple of other officers from B team arrived to give us a hand. I asked them to search the bedrooms. Peter Bleksley came out from one bedroom with a photograph. He asked me what the prisoner's name was, and I told him Richard Rowbotham.

'How do you spell his surname?' he asked.

I said 'Does it matter Peter? Just carry on with the search. Do you know him?'

'You won't believe this, Jock,' he replied. 'That's my girlfriend's bedroom, and that's a picture of her and her brother.'

I felt sorry for him but, being the professional he was, he completed the search.

When the case came up for trial at the Inner London Crown Court, the defence counsel had a field day. They suggested Peter had used Wendy, his girlfriend, to infiltrate her brother's drugs team. This was totally wrong, as Peter had nothing whatsoever to do with the job, and it was a complete coincidence that he happened to answer my call for assistance. However, this was the end of Peter's relationship with Wendy. Rowbotham got four years, and I still have a letter he sent me from prison. Peter was one of our top undercover officers at the Yard. Since he retired he has written at least two books. He mentions the above incident in his book *Gangbuster*.

Another team from the drug squad had for some months been negotiating a deal for the purchase of heroin from a couple of Glasgow hooligans – and believe me they were just that. When the day came to complete the deal all the drug squad officers were involved. The exchange of drugs and money was to take place in a telephone box in Regent's Park

The park was surrounded by officers in all types of vehicles. Peter Bleksley and I were lying on the top floor of a double-decker bus which we had hired for the job. It was parked in the car park and close to where the deal was to take place. We had plenty of troops covering all exits to the park.

The officers dealing with the job from the outset suspected that the Glasgow boys might not have any drugs, but would attempt to rob our team of their money. The bandits turned up four-handed as arranged, and sure enough, as soon as they were shown the money they pulled out a firearm, threatened the officers and demanded the money.

The undercover officers handed over the briefcase, which contained £90,000, knowing that it would soon be recovered by us.

The Glasgow boys scattered in all directions, but Peter and I were able to capture one of them. We had a job detaining him, but we managed to handcuff him and place him in the double-decker bus. If my memory serves me right, a second bandit was run over by a car driven by one our boys and arrested.

The other two got completely away with the briefcase of money. We had the park thoroughly searched, but they were nowhere to be found. My everlasting memory of that job was seeing the new DI we had sitting on the step of the bus with his head in his hands, moaning about his career and the loss of the Commissioner's money.

The briefcase with all the money was eventually found in London Zoo nearby, in a skip where the elephant dung was collected. A couple of weeks later the two robbers who escaped went to visit their mates in prison and they were also captured.

The charge was good stuff: 'That you did rob Davy Crockett, an officer of the Metropolitan Police, of £90,000, the property of the Commissioner.'

We were working on a drugs job up in Harrow Road. It was a beautiful sunny morning and we had had an early morning start to get a good parking spot for our observation van.

Once the van is in position, the person keeping observation inside has to stay there until something happens. Every movement is logged. The van is equipped with dual controls so that from the inside of the back one can operate the lights, windscreen wiper, windows, horn and indicators.

The biggest problem is finding a volunteer to man it. No-one wants to sit in the observation van in hot weather. It gets so hot one has to strip down to underpants. You have to have gallons of water as the body dehydrates. It makes me laugh when I hear of someone being prosecuted for leaving a dog in a car in hot weather. We were no better off than a dog. At that time I was the oldest man on the squad, but as there were no volunteers from the youngsters I did the job myself.

I was in position by 6.30 am. A colleague parked the van, locked up and left me to it. By two o'clock I was starving, and there was still no movement from the target address. I asked over the radio for two McDonalds to be delivered to me. Steve Gaskin duly appeared, and I wound the window down, using the controls in the rear of the van. Steve walked past and threw the box with the burgers inside, then carried on without stopping. Before I could close the window, two black youths came into view. They were looking into all the parked cars. When they came to my van they saw the window was open, and my lunch lying on the seat. They promptly got in the van and got stuck into my feast, the little bastards.

Being a bit bored I thought I would play a little game with them. From my position in the back I switched the wipers on. They just looked at each other and laughed. When I switched the indicators on, they both scratched their heads but carried on munching away. I then lowered the passenger door window. By this time I could see they were concerned, but when I blew the horn they both jumped up and ran off, shouting 'Voodoo! Voodoo!'

The Marcoullis Case

This was one of my best and most satisfying jobs, despite the fact that I was badly let down by colleagues. The following two reports are copies of the actual reports I submitted to senior officers some 33 years ago. I will go into more detail about this case after the reports.

First Report

METROPOLITAN POLICE
CRIMINAL INVESTIGATION DEPARTMENT
New Scotland Yard
16th day of September 1987
Detective Chief Superintendent Penrose

On 10th September 1987, Andrew Christhiou Marcoullis, Age 58, CRO . . . was arrested and charged at Kentish Town Police Station as follows:

On 10th September 1987, within the jurisdiction of the Central Criminal Court, you in contravention of Section 4(1) of the Misuse of Drugs Act, 1971, were concerned in the supply of controlled drugs of Class 'A', mainly heroin, to another.

Contrary to Section 4(3)(b) Misuse of Drugs Act, 1971.

The arrest of this evil drugs dealer was as a direct result of information supplied to me by an informant whose identity is known to Detective Chief Superintendent Penrose, but for the purpose of this report will be known as John FORD.

Marcoullis is the owner of a restaurant at 23, Pratt Street, NW1. Above these premises he had an illegal gaming club. He also had a flat in Finchley Road from where he controlled several prostitutes. Through these premises he supplied a vast area of Central London with heroin, cocaine and a mixture of both commonly known as speedball. This was confirmed by two of his prostitutes who were on the premises when they were searched. About 70 packages were found in the premises which were ready for distribution that night. On top of this police recovered about 8 ozs of cocaine and heroin. It has now been confirmed, MARCOULLIS had 2 kilos of heroin the night before police searched the premises, which was the original information John FORD had supplied.

John FORD has previously been rewarded from the Informants Fund for the information he supplied to me in the recovery of 610 kilos of cannabis. This large quantity of cannabis was at the time the biggest seizure of cannabis by Metropolitan police.

I now ask that this report be forwarded so that John FORD can be suitably rewarded for information he supplied in the arrest of this evil drugs pusher.

John Murray
Detective Constable
S.O.1(4) – Central Drugs Squad

Second Report

METROPOLITAN POLICE
District 4 Area
Station Mitcham
25th July 1988
Re:– Andrew Christhiou MARCOULLIS *CRO . . .*
<u>Detective Chief Superintendent Penrose</u>

With reference to the above quoted correspondence and in particular to the trial of Andrew Chrisathou MARCOULLIS at Snaresbrook Crown Court which commenced on Monday 27th June and finished on Friday 8th July 1988.

The facts of the case are fully set out in correspondence No ——. This correspondence is in the possession of Detective Inspector —— who is attached to SO1 (4).

On 13th January 1988 MARCOULLIS was granted bail with certain conditions. One of those conditions being not to contact any of the witnesses involved in the case.

All the witnesses in the case are prostitutes and drug addicts and from the outset, it was an extremely difficult case to present before a court.

After he got bail, MARCOULLIS contacted one of the witnesses at her home address and invited her to come to his restaurant at 23, Pratt Street, NW1. He gave her heroin and made her write a letter addressed to himself, stating that a statement she made to Detective Constable MURRAY was taken under duress and that the officer had threatened to arrest her if she did not comply.

He then took her to a Solicitor's address in Muswell Hill where he got her to make an affidavit giving the same details as in the aforementioned letter.

He visited this witness in H.M. Prison Holloway under the name GARDINER, 4 days before the Trial and told her not to give evidence for the Prosecution.

As the prosecuting officer I was not aware of his activities until the morning of the trial when the witness who was in custody for a different offence told me. She made a further statement to Police in which she outlined the activities of MARCOULLIS whilst he was on bail. This statement was produced at the Trial.

A second witness attended Court and whilst he was waiting outside the Court room, he was threatened by MARCOULLIS. A statement was obtained from him to this effect. The Learned Judge who tried the Case was informed of these events.

On Friday 8th July, MARCOULLIS was found Guilty of 4 Counts of Possession with intent to supply a 'Controlled Drug'. He was sentenced to 3 years imprisonment. He was ordered to pay £3,000 Costs and £3,000 was forfeited under the Drugs Trafficking Act.

I am pleased to say the Jury believed both witnesses when told MARCOULLIS had interfered with or threatened them. Whilst MARCOULLIS was on bail, I believe he gave information to officers attached to SO1(4), which resulted in some arrests and recovery of a quantity of a restricted drug.

I was informed of this a couple of days before the trial. I was also informed that a letter would be given to the Judge from Police to this effect as is common when such people give information to Police.

As a Police Officer who has served on several squads attached to the Commissioner's Office, I am fully aware that such letters are necessary and that informants of the calibre of MARCOULLIS are a 'necessary evil' when dealing with organised crime.

In view of the fact that MARCOULLIS had interfered

with one of the witnesses, especially when it concerned a statement that I had taken and also that he had threatened witnesses, I felt it was my duty to inform Senior Officers at SO1(4). I suggested that instead of a letter, the fact that he had assisted police could have been said in open Court.

On 20th July 1978 MARCOULLIS gave evidence for the defence at the Central Criminal Court in the case of Vincent HARVEY CRO ——, who was on trial for Living on Immoral Earnings, Grievous Bodily Harm and Rape. Correspondence No —— refers. He was accused by Prosecution Counsel of lying. His reply was 'What about the Metropolitan Police, how many trials have they dropped in the last two months? What about the Football Trials? It was the Metropolitan Police that was lying.'

There is no doubt that MARCOULLIS is an evil man and I feel that if the author of the letter to The Learned Judge at Snaresbrook Crown Court had been made aware of the extreme length he went to, to discredit police evidence during his trial, such a letter would not have been granted.

I strongly feel that an administrative error was made in granting MARCOULLIS a letter and I now ask that this report be forwarded to Commander C1 for his information, with a request that MARCOULLIS informant's file be noted for future reference in order to protect officers in future.

John Murray
Detective Constable
Mitcham Police Station

I was on the Drugs Squad at the yard when I got information that Andrew Marcoullis, who owned a restaurant in Camden Town in North London, was heavily involved in the supply and distribution of drugs, mainly heroin, in that area. After keeping observation for a few days I obtained a search warrant for his premises. We didn't find any drugs, but we did find plenty of evidence that the restaurant had been used in connection with drugs.

I took him to his home address, a flat in Finchley Road, where I discovered rooms that had been used as cages for prostitutes who were addicted to heroin. The doors were actually made of iron bars so he was able to keep an eye on the girls at any one time.

Angela Wilde was a bonny girl from a decent family who had unfortunately become addicted to heroin. To feed her habit, Angela had turned to prostitution, and she and three other girls worked for Marcoullis, who was their pimp. He fed them with heroin, and the money they earned from prostitution he kept for himself. The girls told me all this in statements I took from them, and they agreed to give evidence for the prosecution.

Marcoullis was charged and appeared in court. He applied for bail on four occasions, but I managed to keep him in custody. Before a date was set for his trial, I was transferred back to Division. He again applied for bail in my absence, and it was granted on condition he did not contact any of the witnesses in the case. I was not told this.

On the morning of the trial, Angela Wilde was taken to court in a prison van as she was serving a sentence for another offence. She was the only one of the prostitutes to turn up. I went to see her in the cells and she told me the following story.

After Marcoullis was granted bail, he telephoned her at her home address. He invited her round to his place where he gave her some heroin. He then made her withdraw the statement she had previously made to me. He did the same to all the witnesses I had interviewed. He also took her to a solicitor, where an affidavit was taken from her. Angela was still under the influence of drugs, and she signed the affidavit which said I had taken the original statement under duress.

That morning in court was the first time I found out about this. I persuaded Angela to make a further statement where she reiterated the story she had told me. This was handed to the Prosecuting Counsel, who in turn told the Judge. The trial went on as scheduled. Angela was called as a witness, and she performed brilliantly in the witness box. She was the only witness

I had left, and I would have lost the case if it wasn't for her. I could have kissed her, prostitute or no prostitute, when the foreman of the jury said 'Guilty'.

Having had all this hassle, I was more than surprised when ex-colleagues from the Drug Squad handed the Judge a letter to say Marcoullis had been helpful to police. This was despite the fact that he had made extremely serious allegations against me. He was also in breach of his bail conditions, in that he had interfered with witnesses. I had worked on many jobs with one of the officers who handed the letter to the judge, and I felt really, really let down. I have never spoken to him since.

The Judge had obviously seen through this wicked bastard and was of the same opinion as me. Despite the letter, he sentenced Marcoullis to three years in prison, ordered him to pay £3,000 costs and forfeited a further £3,000.

Two weeks after he was sentenced, Marcoullis was produced from prison at the Central Criminal Court to give evidence on behalf of another major criminal. He made serious allegations against police in that case too. We could not operate without informants, but we could do without informants like Marcoullis.

I got more satisfaction from this job than any other job I had throughout my service. As Angela was in prison at the time I was not able to thank her properly for standing up in the witness box to give evidence against that wicked and evil man.

It is a custom within the CID that we all have a drink after a successful prosecution in a major case. On this occasion it gave me great pleasure to stick two fingers up at the officers who tried to get Marcoullis off the hook. I was proud of the hard work I put in and of the end result.

Cannabis Haul

Throughout the years I served at the Yard, there was friction between the police and officers of Her Majesty's Customs and Excise. This was caused by a ruling that all drug import operations were to be handed to HM Customs. When it comes to drugs, everyone knows heroin, cocaine and large amounts of cannabis are at some stage imported. If the drugs have already arrived on our shores then the police can deal with them, but if the drugs are on their way into the country then it's a case for Customs to handle.

John Ford came up trumps again. He supplied me with the names of two Greek Cypriots living in the London area, who were about to import a large amount of cannabis. Ford was specific about the method to be used in the importation. The slabs of cannabis were going to be hidden amongst a cargo of oranges.

The targets were followed for several days, and we finally located a warehouse used by them in North London. I anticipated this was the warehouse the shipment was to be delivered to. Once this was established, I decided there was no point in continuing to follow them, as there was always the possibility they would suss us.

Unfortunately, we could not find a suitable place to keep observation close to the warehouse. Accordingly, I hired a tent which I set up on the roof of a 12-storey block of flats. It was an ideal place but cold. I was very reluctant to tell Customs, as it was my job and my information. I had done the nitty-gritty stuff and I was quite capable of dealing with it myself. When I informed senior officers at the Yard, they told me I *had to* inform Customs, as it was an importation. I argued that all drugs were imported, but to no avail. Reluctantly, I did as I was told and a joint operation with Customs was mounted

A few days later a lorry arrived with a cargo of oranges in crates. We let the targets do all the hard work unloading the van, then as they finished, we raided the warehouse and arrested four conspirators. We seized 601 kilos of cannabis, which at the time was the biggest seizure of cannabis made by the Metropolitan Police.

I was still annoyed that I had had to tell Customs. I had nothing against custom officers but there was always a bit of needle when we worked together.

My Last Buy Job on Drugs Work

On Friday 23 August 1985, I was hoping to slide off early because I was taking my family for a weekend down on the coast. As I was leaving Scotland Yard I met Mickey Green, a DC on another squad. He looked pretty excited, with a big smile on his face. He called me over and told me he had an urgent buy job coming off as soon as he could find someone to do the buy for him. 'Can you do it, Jock?' he asked, 'I'll buy you a dram' – as if it would take a dram to convince me to do it!

I agreed, but told him I wanted to get away as soon as possible. 'No problem,' said Mickey, 'It will be all over by 3 o'clock.'

Mickey gave me a sample of cocaine he had taken possession of from the informant. I was then introduced to the informant, a man I now knew as Mohamed. He took me to King's Cross Railway Station, where we arrived at 1 pm. We waited in the street by the cab rank.

At 1.50 pm, Mohamed met two Arabic men, one of whom was in tribal clothing. He had a conversation with them away from me. When he came back to me with the two other men, he introduced me to them as 'John'. He introduced the smaller of the two men to me as Ajas, but I cannot remember the name of the second man.

There was a conversation between them in a foreign language.

I said to Ajas, 'I thought you were going to meet me at one o'clock – it's now ten to two. What the hell do you think you're playing at?'

'Sorry, Mr John,' he said, 'it's the trains – you know the guards are on a go-slow.'

'When I do business I expect you to be on time,' I said.

'Yes,' he replied, 'I promise I will be next time.'

'That sample you gave me is not good,' I told him. 'How much are you asking per kilo?'

'How much do you want to give?' was his reponse.

At this point I gave Mohamed money to buy cigarettes and coffee and he left.

I said to Ajas, 'No more than £14,000 – the gear is shit.'

Ajas spoke to the man in tribal clothing in a foreign language, then he turned back to me and said, 'OK, he is happy with that.'

I said, 'I've got the money here – do you want to see it?'

Ajas shook his head. 'No, I believe you.'

'How many kilos can you supply?' I asked.

'Only one this time, as this is the first time we have done business.'

'I was told you could do five kilos,' I protested, 'what the fuck are you playing at?'

He said, 'Next week we will have plenty.'

'But my man's got money out of the bank for five kilos,' I went on. 'He may not want to buy one kilo. We've come down from Scotland for this.'

Ajas spoke to the man in tribal clothing, then told me, 'My friend is going back home to Afghanistan tomorrow and needs the money for the kilo today.'

'I'm not sure if my man will take just a kilo,' I said, 'as he has other contacts. Where is the gear now? Will you deliver it today?'

He spoke to the tribal man again and said, 'Yes, we will have it here by 6 o'clock. It's not far away.'

'I will speak to my man first and see if he will accept a kilo. He might want to wait until next week for a big parcel. I will see you back here at 3.15.'

'OK, Mr John, I will see you then at quarter past three.'

I left them there and went to King's Cross Police Station, where I made notes.

When I returned to King's Cross Railway Station at 3.15 pm, I saw the three men again.

I said to Ajas, 'My man will have the kilo, but he is not happy travelling from Scotland for one kilo. He wants to weigh it before he parts with the dough.'

Ajas said, 'Yes, that's OK. When can you do that?'

'He is arranging for a room at the Royal Scot Hotel just down the road,' I replied. 'What time will you be back?'

He looked at the train timetable and said, 'I will try and make it for six o'clock.'

'My man will be with me,' I said, 'and he will want to see the gear.'

'OK, Mr John,' he agreed, 'six o'clock.'

Again I returned to Scotland Yard to make notes.

Bill Lyons, another Scotsman, was to act as 'Mr Big' with the money. We took a taxi to King's Cross, arriving at 6.20 pm. The man in tribal dress was standing in the station by the entrance to the underground. We approached him and I said, 'Where is the gear?'

In broken English he replied, 'He won't be long – train late.'

We stayed with him for a few minutes talking about cricket and hockey, which he told us he played. He then said, 'I will go and look,' and left us.

At 6.30 pm he returned. 'OK, he will not be long.'

'I will wait until seven o'clock,' I said, 'and then I am off.'

He then left us, and Bill Lyons and I had coffee in the station cafe.

It was almost seven o'clock when Ajas came up to me carrying a briefcase.

I said, 'I don't like this. You said six and now it is seven. There are police patrolling, and they have been watching us.'

'It's all right, Mr John,' he said, 'It's the trains.'

The man in tribal clothing and DC Lyons joined us and I introduced them. 'This is Bill. He's the man with the money.'

Ajas then handed the briefcase to the man in tribal clothing and said to him, 'Go round the corner with him.' He and Bill went round the corner and out of our view.

'Next week we will have plenty white powder,' Ajas said.

'Let's get this one out of the way first,' I replied. 'I'm not sure if we want to deal with you any more. I like to keep times because police know me, and they will give me a pull if they see me hanging around.'

DC Lyon and the man returned.

'It's there,' said Bill, 'let's go to the hotel.' We started walking down Euston Road.

At this stage everything went wrong. The arrangement we had made was that as soon as Bill Lyons had seen the drugs and come back to the group, he would blow his nose into a red handkerchief. This would be the signal for a swoop to arrest. Unfortunately the radio of the unit member who was keeping eyeball on us failed. He tried to get through to the others but they were not getting a signal.

The four of us, Bill Lyons and I, together with the two Arabs, were approaching the hotel. Still there was no movement from our team. There was no room booked in the Royal Scot. We were getting too close for my liking, and I was beginning to think Bill and I would have to do the arrest ourselves. Thankfully our team arrived just in time, and as they did, Bill and I did a runner.

The above is based on the evidence I gave at the Old Bailey. This buy was the easiest one I ever did. The Arabs were not professionals by any means. They were all convicted and got four years. However, they caused me a lot of problems afterwards by making a complaint which was investigated by the Complaints Department at Scotland Yard. This investigation went on for over a year. Their story was that they were selling diamonds to me, not drugs. They alleged that they handed me a bag of diamonds and that I swapped it for a bag of drugs.

This was not the first family weekend spoilt thanks to Mickey Green, but for this one he still owes me a dram.

Hassling Tiddler

When serving on the drug squad, as indeed on most squads, one spends half the time waiting, watching and following. On one particular job we were liaising with police from the continent, who were following an international team of drugs couriers carrying a large quantity of drugs. They were bound for London. Drugs barons do an enormous amount of planning when working out a route to the UK. Continental police were in communication with officers at the Yard who relayed the information to us by radio. One minute we were told the drug dealers were about to board in Paris, next they were en route to Amsterdam and so on.

I could never get tired of an observation at London Airport, because there is so much to see and so many different faces and nationalities. It is incredible that there are no two faces alike.

Now, back near the start of this book I mentioned fellow islander John MacLeod, who was nicknamed 'Tiddler'. As we were waiting for instructions, I was sitting in an observation platform when I saw our Tiddler coming in from abroad. I knew he would have at least a couple of bottles of whisky. I got on the radio and gave his description and asked for him to be stopped. Colleagues argued over the radio that he was not one of our targets. I just told them he was one of mine and to search his suitcase.

This they did, then came back and reported, 'He's clean, Jock – just a couple of bottles of whisky on him.' I told them to hang on to him until I came down.

When I got to the arrival lounge, there was poor Tiddler standing there looking pretty confused. As I approached him I could see the look of relief on his face. He knew I was a serving police officer. I asked him what was wrong, and told me he had been stopped going through the green channel. He had nothing to declare and he was being detained for no reason.

I said, 'Tiddler, tell the truth. You have two bottles of whisky and do you think you are going through the airport without buying me a drink?'

'You bastard, Jock!' was his response.

We retired to an adjoining office where we discussed his latest trip in reclining chairs with a wee dram. I can honestly say he didn't have two bottles when he left. This was 30 years ago and we still laugh about it when we meet.

A Car Dealer and Killer

In August 1971 I bought a Singer Vogue estate from a car front in Tooting, South London. It really was one of the best cars I ever owned.

A week later a Police Superintendent, Gerry Richardson, was murdered. A team of five armed robbers entered Preston's Jewellers in the Strand, Blackpool. They held up the staff in the front of the shop, but they did not realise there was a member of staff in the back room. He pressed the silent alarm which went directly to Blackpool Police Station. The call was answered by Supt Richardson and colleagues and a high-speed chase took place.

The team split up. Supt Richardson captured the main man, who was identified as 'Fat Freddie' Sewell, but Sewell grabbed the Superintendent by the throat and shot him at point-blank range in the stomach. Fat Freddie Sewell was none other than the car dealer I had just bought my Singer Vogue from a week earlier. The robbery team involved all came from London. Their names were circulated via the *Police Gazette*. I contacted the Blackpool murder squad and told them about my car, but there was little else I could tell them. I am pleased to say Sewell and his team received a total of 90 years in prison. He was released in 2001, having served 30 years.

14

My Last Posting

I left the drugs squad in 1987 and was posted to Mitcham. It was a posting nearer my home so I was quite happy. Little did I know then it was to be my last posting.

We had a keep-fit fanatic of a sergeant, Stuart Sutherland. Stuart came in one morning and accused everyone in the office of being overweight. One did not have to be a detective to form this opinion. I for one was certainly overweight.

It was decided we would all go to the gym twice a week under the supervision of Stuart. It cost me a fortune, as I bought a new bike, a new tracksuit, new trainers and a new bag to carry all this gear.

The first morning of our schedule I got all dressed in my sporty rig-out and set out on my bike. I was flashing past all the cars stopped in traffic jams between Sutton and Mitcham. I had been doing this journey by car for the past 20-odd years, and it gave me great pleasure to knock on the roofs of the cars as I cycled past. I could imagine the drivers thinking, 'Hell, that's Jock! He must be off his trolley.'

I met the rest of the group at the gym as arranged, and Stuart soon had us running around like blue-assed flies. Press-ups, lift-ups, back-ups – you mention it, he had us doing it.

Then we came to weightlifting. Stuart grabbed the weights and lifted them above his head quite easily. I thought, 'You flash bastard! I can do that.'

By this time I was completely knackered, but I was not prepared to let Stuart show off and do something no one else could do, so I stuck out my chest and grabbed the weights. This was to be the last weights I ever lifted. I got them as far as my waist and could not get them any further.

I suddenly felt awful, but rather than lose face I told them I was going for a pint at the Queen's Head. I must have been feeling really rough as I actually walked past the pub and straight to the office. I bumped into the typist who told me I looked terrible.

I had arranged for my wife Donalda to bring my suit in to the office as I was late turn that day. I went and sat in the toilet until she arrived. I didn't have any pain as such, but felt as if someone was squeezing me really hard.

At quarter to two Donalda drove into the station yard with my suit and shirt ready for my shift, and I went down to meet her. She didn't ask me any questions, she just said, 'Jump in', and drove off.

'Hey, what's up darling?' I asked.

She said, 'I'm taking you straight to hospital,' and she did.

I had all sorts of wires attached to me, and it was diagnosed that I had suffered a heart attack. For the next two days I was in intensive care with my new tracksuit, wearing it as my pyjamas. So much for Stuart and his keep-fit!

I was off work for three months, the longest spell I ever spent with the family. By the end of that time they were all pleased to get rid of me.

I went back to work on light duties, but it was not for me. On 21 November 1989 I left the service, but not before a farewell party which was attended by over 200 family and friends.

I can say I never passed an exam while I was a serving officer. Every January a promotion exam was held in Sarah Siddons School in Paddington. It was an excellent day out for me. I never ever studied because I was too busy working. When I was a young Aide to CID you *had* to take the exam, otherwise you were sent back to uniform. On the day of the exam you had to stay in the classroom for at least 20 minutes. After that, the ones who were there just for a reunion would give the signal to each other and meet at a prearranged pub venue. I usually got home on the last train. My records show I took the exam eight times without passing it. Looking back now, I envy my colleagues who are on a much higher pension than me.

I was happy in the police, very happy, and enjoyed it most of the time. I came across many who were lazy, some very lazy, some who talked a great job in the pub but never had a job of their own. I came across many who served in supposedly elite squads who never ever stood in the witness box and gave evidence, and were there only because of their affiliation to some secret society or other. I have served on nearly all the specialised squads at Scotland Yard. It is a myth to say that a squad officer is a better officer than his divisional CID colleague. We all had to start on Division, and I know many good divisional CID officers who for one reason or other never served on a squad. Quite often it was 'not what you know but who you know'.

One thing that did annoy me was that when we as a squad worked hard, worked all sorts of hours, put ourselves on offer, and then our overtime was cut, when at the same time uniform officers who were stationed at Buckingham Palace, Downing Street and the Houses of Parliament were earning twice as much for being glorified security guards.

Hebridean Colleagues

There were several Hebridean senior officers who came from the croft and humble beginnings and achieved positions of high rank within the Met during my time.

John Morrison finished as Assistant Commissioner (Crime). I have a photograph of him and the black house where he was born and a full history of his career.

Alex Morrison, Chief Superintendent, went to Scotland as Chief Constable of Grampian and finished as HM Inspector of Constabulary for Scotland.

John MacIver, who became Detective Superintendent and Commandant of the Detective Training School.

Finlay MacLennan, Chief Superintendent, transferred to Scotland as Assistant Chief Constable of Northern Counties.

Donald Smith, Chief Superintendent, came from Uist.

Commissioners' Commendations

Here are some of the commendations I picked up for my work with the police.

28 March 1969
Commended for 'Perseverance and Ability', leading to the arrest of a team for pick-pocketing.

21 November 1969
For 'Initiative and Ability', leading to the arrest of a team for stealing £52,000 from parking meters.

4 December 1970
For 'Persistence and Ability', leading to arrests for conspiracy and theft.

1 February 1971
For 'Initiative and Ability', leading to arrests for burglary.

23 June 1972
For 'Courage and Determination' in the face of possession of a firearm.

6 August 1976
For 'Persistence and Ability', leading to arrests for burglary and possession of firearms.

7 December 1978
For 'Persistence and Detective Ability', leading to arrests for burglary and possession of firearms.

21 March 1980
For 'Outstanding Dedication and Devotion to Duty' in a case of armed robbery. Also commended at Maidstone Crown Court.

8 June1982
For 'Diligence and Dedication' in a case of murder.

9 August 1985
For 'Professionalism' in a case of conspiracy and possession of firearms and drugs.

Here is a selection of senior officers' assessments and comments on my work:

'A mature man, dependable, loyal. A practical man who has a good success with crime arrests.' Kenneth Newman, Superintendant, 1965 (later Sir Kenneth Newman, Commissioner).

'A good solid, mature officer, shows determination to success in his chosen career. He retains his native tongue, which can sometimes be difficult to follow.' William Little, Detective Chief Inspector, 1967.

'This officer impressed by his strength and honesty of purpose.' Staff at Detective Training School, Walton Street, 1968.

'A good detective who is extremely conscientious and loyal.' Michael O'Neil, Detective Chief Superintendent, 1969.

'This officer kicked about the world in the Merchant Navy and as a whaler; the experience has given him a reliability and loyalty which cannot be faulted.' Detective Chief Superintendent Ivor Reynolds, 1970.

'A big, strong, rugged individual from the Scottish Isles. Always willing to assist his colleagues and most firm in dealing with any member of the criminal fraternity.' Detective Chief Superintendent Bennett, 1974.

'A family man who is extremely fond of his children.' Detective Inspector Joe Bell, 1975.

'A large, fearsome Scot.' Detective Chief Superintendent Reg Lasham, 1976.

'A dour Scot who is completely dedicated to his job. He

has five children to whom he is devoted.' Detective Chief Superintendent Randall Jones, 1978.

'Not exactly placid, an excellent interrogator, abounds with energy and gives his all to the service. His reliability is beyond reproach. He is at his best when dealing with the professional armed robber, as I have seen him do over the past nine months on Operation "Ohio".' Detective Chief Inspector Bill Forman, 1979.

'He organises, controls and guides with the force of a tornado. A first class detective officer who leads from the front. Meticulous in his preparation, a determined man who at all times strives for perfection in the detection of offenders.' Detective Chief Inspector Leslie Bell, 1984.

'A man who in his 25th year gives outstanding commitment to his work. A family man.' Detective Chief Superintendent William MacLaurin, 1987.

'This high assessment of Detective Constable Murray's contribution to the Metropolitan Police is a testament to our high regard for this officer. Although long in service, he never fails to give his all.' Detecive Chief Inspector Brian Tompkins on the day I retired in 1989.

15

After the Police Force

Having been looked after for the past 27 years, I now had to adjust to the idea of another job. I didn't want to work for anyone else again. However, I did apply for a job that was advertised in one of the police magazines. This was as a Chief Security Advisor to Cadbury, the famous confectionery manufacturer. I arrived at their office in Bourneville, Birmingham, with another 20 or so who had also applied. I recognised several faces of officers from the rank of Commander downwards, and I was certainly the lowest in rank.

We were given a test paper to fill out, and it was all ticking boxes. I had never sat this type of exam before, but I decided to give it a try. I think we had two hours to complete the paper. Commonsense was all that was needed and time taken to study the question. After something like three-quarters of an hour, a lot of the ones I recognised as senior officers in the past had completed the paper and were off. I was still on the second question!

'What chance have I got?' I thought. Anyway, I stuck it out and was still writing when the two hours were up. I was the only one left in the room.

Two days later I had a call from Cadbury to say they were offering me the job. I was absolutely delighted to know I had been chosen before those who had so recently been my senior officers. That was one exam I was truly pleased to pass.

However, I decided not to accept the job. Cadbury's were disappointed and offered me an extra £2,000 on top of the salary it was advertised for, but I declined. As I mentioned, I had vowed I would never work for anyone else again. I recommended an ex-colleague from the Flying Squad, Roger Driscoll, to them. Roger got the job and stayed there for many years.

Asset Investigations

The first thing I did after leaving the police was to form my own company, 'Asset Investigations', and the second was to recruit someone who I believed to be one of the most dedicated CID officers I had worked with, Norman Vatcher. Over the next six years Norman was a pillar of strength, and I often relied on him in the most difficult situations.

I had signed a contract with a reputable investigation company called Linden Management Services. They wanted me to do all their surveillance work. This was up my street, as surveillance was part of my work on squads for many years. I will always be grateful to Linden Management, as they gave me the opportunity to start up on my own as Asset Investigations, which was very, very successful. I even did work for Cadburys eventually.

One of the best and hardest jobs I had with Linden Management concerned a certain Russell Causley, who had taken out a life insurance policy for a large amount, something in the region of £750,000. A few months later he was reported missing, having been lost overboard from a yacht. Apparently he had been sailing off Guernsey with his common-law wife Patricia and another couple, when he fell overboard and drowned. His body was never found.

When a claim was made for the insurance money, the insurance company was not happy and Linden Management instructed me to look into the matter. We had information that Patricia Causley was coming into Heathrow Airport on a given date and we decided to follow her to see if she would make contact with her husband, if he was still alive.

The day she arrived was the rainiest I had ever seen in London. I had two vehicles and a motorbike for the operation. Just as her flight arrived, everything went wrong. My van reversed into the motorbike, putting both vehicles out of commission. This left me on my own.

She was seen getting into a taxi which I managed to follow. She sat in the rear seat of the cab, and not once did she look ahead. She deliberately sat in a position which enabled her to look out of the back for the duration of the journey, obviously to see if anyone was coming behind her. These were the actions of someone who had something to hide. I followed her to a hotel close to Heathrow.

For the next few months we tailed her. She knew we were doing this, and several times she drove straight into police stations in the Kent and Sussex area to complain. She was a difficult cookie to follow and kept moving address. On one occasion we tracked her to a house in the middle of nowhere. The only place where we could keep observation on it was from a nearby ditch. It was a cold winter, one of the few winters when we had snow in the London area.

Eventually she met up with her husband who was arrested and sentenced to two years in prison. She was given a suspended sentence of 12 months for conspiracy to defraud.

While he was serving his sentence Russell Causley confided in fellow cellmates. One day he said to them that the date was the best day of his life and he always celebrated it. He then told them it was the day he had murdered his wife. He was arrested, charged, convicted of her murder and sentenced to 16 years.

A friend of mine from the Isle of Lewis phoned me one day to say an Irish colleague of his had been arrested by officers from HM Customs for an income tax fraud, and he wanted me to act on his behalf. At the time I was aware that subcontractors in the construction industry were involved in a huge scam involving tax. If my memory serves me right, this was to do with a form, 714, issued to subcontractors enabling them to deduct income tax from payments by the main contractor and to send it direct to HM Customs.

Again, if my memory serves me right, what the Irishman was

doing was buying blank 714 forms from other subbies, filling the forms in as if the tax had been deducted from the main contractor's payments, but actually pocketing the tax himself.

The amount of money he was accused of obtaining fraudulently came to about half a million pounds. I went through the case papers with the Irishman, and realised there was one witness missing whom the Customs officers had not interviewed and without whom they would lose the case. It was also blatantly obvious that the Irishman was engaged in a massive fraud. I found it very hard to act on behalf of a person who I knew not to be innocent, having spent the past 27 years flogging my guts out prosecuting the guilty.

The Irishman was offering me good money if I could get him off the charges against him. I agreed to act on his behalf. I made numerous enquiries amongst the Irish subcontractors in the London area, and soon realised I was dealing with the most devious members of the building trade. I had stumbled upon a massive, massive fraud which was worked nationwide. I stuck to the case of the one Irishman who had hired me, and passed the information I got on others to the police.

I traced the man I wanted, the missing witness, to an address in Hull, and when I called on him I could see he was absolutely gobsmacked. He thought I was police and asked how I had managed to trace him. I explained to him I was no longer a police officer but was acting as a private investigator for the Irishman who I believed had purchased some blank 714 forms from him. He agreed he had sold them. He told me he was aware the Customs were after him, and to avoid capture he had joined the French Foreign Legion, where he served for three years. He had only been back in the country for a week before I found him.

I took a statement from him which was served on HM Customs. The charges against the Irishman were dropped. I couldn't believe my ears when the counsel acting for the Irishman asked for costs, which the learned judge awarded. Not only did the Irishman get away scot free, he was able to claim all the money he had spent on his defence, including my costs.

I felt more guilt myself for getting him off the hook than the Irishman himself, whom I knew to be guilty. I still cannot fathom out how a defence solicitor or QC can congratulate themselves on their success in getting a guilty client off on a charge like murder or rape.

Other Scams

Black cab taxi drivers have a special insurance that covers them when they are off sick or injured. Many take advantage of this and from time to time abuse it. Linden Management instructed me to investigate one particular driver who had been claiming for years.

At the time I had a girl called Fiona working for me. She was an excellent operator. We arrived outside the driver's address at 6 am, to find the taxi was parked on the drive. My plan was that if the target drove the taxi away I would drop her off and she would hail the taxi and instruct the driver to take her to meet her boss at London Airport.

Everything went according to plan. The target picked her up and off we went. He was delighted with the fare and was even more delighted when she got to the airport and asked him to wait for her and take her back into London. She took him to Belgravia where she met me.

I asked him if he could stay with us for the rest of the day, which he agreed to do. Fiona and I had lunch with John, a rich friend of mine. Afterwards we gave John a lift to his office and then we went back to London Airport. Quite the most relaxing job I ever had. It may have cost the insurance company £1,000 for the day, but what would it have cost them had he continued to claim?

I saved insurance companies millions of pounds in claims. A typical example was of a scaffolder who was knocked over by a car in the Old Kent Road, London. He was claiming £1,000,000 from the car insurance company. He even gave his mother power of attorney, as he was supposed to be brain-damaged. However, we suspected he was working.

I had a hell of a job tracing him, because he never slept in the same house two nights on the trot. He moved to different addresses all over southeast London. Once Norman Vatcher and I had housed him we had to follow him to an address, make sure he was in bed, and be up early the next morning to cover him leaving the address.

Eventually we followed him to a building site in Crystal Palace. I found an ideal parking place from which to video him and we watched him erecting scaffolding for the best part of two hours. He was not happy with our vehicle and came over to have a look. He tried all the doors and peered in through my one-way windows. Meanwhile I continued to video and could see the fillings in his teeth. I left the site and at a later date returned with a different vehicle. We were able to video him dismantling three floors of scaffolding in the same day.

On 22 September 1992 I wrote to Peter Lilley, who at the time was Secretary of State for Social Services, and offered to prosecute on behalf of the Ministry people who were claiming unemployment benefit and were at the same time working. He promised he would look into it but I never heard any more.

Retirement

After I retired, we were on holiday in Portugal with friends. We shared a luxurious villa with swimming pool, BBQ and all the mod cons. When the holiday rep was booking us in, she warned us there had been a spate of burglaries in the area.

On our first day we all decided to have dinner in a restaurant. While everyone got dressed I just sat by the pool reading. My wife kept telling me to hurry, but I told her I had no intention of going with them.

'What are you going to do, then?' she asked.

I told her I was going to catch the burglars so that we could all sleep soundly at night. They all laughed and thought I was joking, then duly off they went to dinner.

There was a fig tree in the garden which made an ideal place for observation. As it got dark I got a half-bottle of whisky, a can of cold beer, a glass and a frying pan and took up position under the tree. The frying pan was for protection as I was sure the burglars would be armed with some sort of weapon. It would serve as a shield in the case of an attack on me.

The lights were switched off in the villa and everything was quiet. After about an hour I saw them. Two men in their early twenties came creeping over the fence and were about to break into our villa. I shouted and swore at them and went after them with my frying pan. They really did shit themselves and headed for the hedge.

The rest of our party had just finished dinner and were making their way back to the villa. My wife heard shouting and told the others she thought it was me. At the same time the two burglars jumped the hedge and landed on the pavement directly in front of my wife and the rest of our party. Seconds later 'Jock the Whale' came flying over the hedge, frying pan in hand.

Both burglars were armed, one with a knuckleduster and the other with a knife that had a seven-inch blade. I gave them each a few thumps over the head with my frying pan, and we sat on them until the local police arrived and arrested them. I made a statement to police and was hoping to get a free trip back to Portugal to give evidence, but they pleaded guilty to 26 burglaries throughout the Algarve and my evidence was not required.

Move to Stornoway

Before I retired from the police both my grandfather's croft and my parents' croft went on the market. My mother moved to a flat in Stornoway and my elderly auntie went into a home. My eldest daughter Catriona took a year off after completing her training as a nurse in St Thomas's Hospital, London. She went up to Stornoway where she met her husband David, married and never came back to London again. I was in a position to give her my grandfather's croft as a wedding present and I was delighted it was kept in the family.

In 1996 I saw that one of the local pubs in Stornoway was up for sale. I noticed it was the bank that was selling it and the price was reduced by £80,000. I put a silly offer in for it, not for one moment thinking it would be accepted. A fortnight later I had a solicitor's letter to say my offer was accepted, and of course if one puts an offer in writing in Scotland that makes it legally binding.

I thought, 'Oh shit! What have I done now? And how do I tell Donalda? She hates pubs.'

I didn't say anything to her for a few days, then one night as we lay in bed I whispered in her ear, 'How do you fancy moving to Scotland?'

'I don't mind at all,' she replied, 'sounds a good idea to me. Why have you decided to do this all of a sudden?'

'Well,' I said and coughed, 'I have just bought a pub in Stornoway.'

'Wha . . . wha . . . what did you say?' was her reaction.

I told her what I had done and how it came about and apologised.

After 30-odd years with me she was used to surprises, such as the time I put a report into the Inspector, without her knowledge, asking to be moved from the police flat we were living in to a police house. I put in the report that she was brought up on a croft in the outer Hebrides (she actually had lived in flats in Hendon), and because of this she was allergic to heavy traffic, that she was scared of heights (we were on the first floor) and that she was suffering from depression.

Unknown to me the Inspector went to see her to offer his support.

'How are you feeling today, Mrs Murray?' he asked her.

She said, 'I'm feeling fine.'

He went on, 'How often do you see the doctor?'

By this time she was quite puzzled as to what his motive was. She asked, 'What makes you think I am attending the doctor?'

He said, 'Well, your husband put this report in,' and he let her read my report. She just said, 'Rubbish! Wait until I see him!'

The Inspector laughed his head off and said, 'I can't imagine Jock married to a lunatic.'

The report served its purpose, however, as two months later we got a police house in Sutton, Surrey.

By the time the pub saga came up, all the family, apart from our youngest, Alasdair, had left home. I felt sorry for him, dragging him away from his friends and his brothers and sisters who were still living close to our home in Sutton.

The day before we were due to leave Sutton, I noticed a brand new Mercedes driven by a black man who had recently moved into our road. I had my suspicions about it and did a few checks. I found out the car was wanted by the finance company. I made contact with them and they confirmed that they urgently wanted to recover it. They wanted to find out where the car was, and I told them it was on the other side of London. I negotiated a fee of £500, to which they agreed.

The following morning I kept observation on it from my front room. I saw the driver getting into it. I waved him down and told him he had a flat tyre. When he got out I took possession of the ignition key and told him the car was mine now. I could have done without what happened next. I spent the rest of the day (when I should have been packing) sitting in the car making sure the man was not able to drive it away with a spare key. The fee for recovering the car paid for the furniture removal van.

We had lived in Sutton for nearly 40 years, the happiest days of our lives. One can live in London for years and not speak to some of the neighbours, but on two occasions I arranged street parties. One party was for VE Day, and the second for the Queen's Jubilee. The local constabulary closed the road to traffic. Everybody in our road got involved, and there were tables with food in the middle of the road. Flags decorated the street and we had games for the children. I collected a group of Chelsea Pensioners from Royal Hospital, Chelsea. They certainly needed their walking sticks when we delivered them back to the hospital, plastered.

I had a lump in my throat the day we left for Scotland. Donalda was a lot more composed than me. We were leaving four of our kids and we were leaving the best neighbours one could wish for. We had done so much to the house over the years.

The next time I went to London for our annual retired CID officer's dinner I mistakenly gave my old address to the taxi driver. He dropped me off outside the house, and I spent about 20 minutes trying to get in before I noticed several Chinese faces peering out through the curtains. It was a Chinese family that bought the house from us.

The first thing I did when I took over the pub was change its name to 'The Whaler's'. I did this in memory of the boys I served with in the Antarctic. There was an article in the *News of the World* and soon afterwards people from the Greenpeace organisation paid me a visit. They were not happy with what I was doing, so I changed the name to The Whaler's Rest. I told them the whaler had come home to rest and that I was now against killing whales. They were quite happy with my explanation.

The fun began as soon as I opened the doors to the pub. Within a few weeks I had my own whisky, 'The Whaler's Dram', and this was sold all over the world. My first run-in with the church came when I applied for a Sunday licence. The Isle of Lewis is predominantly Protestant, whilst the southern isles, South Uist and Barra, are Catholic. The Western Isles Licensing Board were granting a Sunday licence to the southern isles, but refusing to give the same to Lewis. I believed this was discrimination of the highest order. Needless to say, they refused my first application.

I had a 70-seat restaurant, so I applied for a table licence on a Sunday. This was granted, and when I opened the doors on Sundays there was a long queue waiting to get in.

Entrance to the restaurant was first come, first served. As long as I served the customer in the restaurant with food I could sell them alcohol, but to get to the restaurant one had to pass through my lounge bar. When the restaurant was full, the ones who were waiting stayed in the lounge bar until there was space in the restaurant.

Half an hour after opening, the lounge bar was full of customers, but I could not serve them. They could be there all day and not get a drink. It got worse when the ones in the restaurant started goading their friends in the lounge. This situation could only happen in Stornoway.

After a couple of weeks I gave in and served the people in the lounge. Everyone was happy, especially me, as the dosh was rolling in. Apart from traffic offences I am not a person who knowingly breaks the law. While in this case I was well aware I was breaking the law, at the same time I was of the opinion the Western Isles Licensing Board were also breaking the law.

After a couple more weeks I decided to go and speak to the local Police Commander, Angus MacLeod. Angus is a gentleman who was only weeks away from retirement. I told him I was breaking the law and I told him what I was doing wrong.

He scratched his head and just said, 'What do you want me to do?'

'Raid me,' I said.

He shook his head and said, 'I am just about to retire and in all my service I have never heard of anyone coming into a police station and asking police to raid him.'

I just replied, 'Angus, I retired from the police eight years ago and I have never heard of anything like it myself.' I was aware this would be a pain in the ass for the police, as they would have to take samples of the drinks and statements from all or most of the customers in the lounge if they did raid me.

The day of reckoning arrived. I was stopped and breathalysed on my way home in the afternoon. I was clear. In the evening a show of force never before seen on a Sunday in Stornoway arrived in my lounge bar. The boys in blue performed their task to the letter, and I had no complaint.

I was summonsed and appeared before the Sheriff Court in Stornoway. I didn't feel uncomfortable in the dock as I had been in so many docks beforehand, but handcuffed to prisoners. I just smiled to myself and reminisced about days gone by.

I pleaded guilty to four charges of serving drinks in the wrong room and was fined £2,000. This was the best investment I ever made, as a couple of weeks later I was granted a Sunday licence. The raid made the national press with the headlines, 'Honest Jock'.

There were no Sunday papers to be had on Lewis, as there were no Sunday flights or Sunday ferry. When Sunday flights started and the first one was due to come from Inverness, I went over to the mainland, booked my ticket and came back with 100 Sunday papers.

There was a big demonstration by the church to greet me at the airport, which certainly got me the publicity I was wanting. My pub was full of newspaper reporters, and the papers were all sold within the hour.

I made arrangements with a shop in Inverness to ship papers over to me every Sunday. I had to pay for the freight myself. The papers were selling well, but I noticed that some people were buying papers and not buying a drink. I soon put a stop to this. I announced that I would not sell a paper to anyone unless they bought a nip and a half-pint. Good days even on a Sunday.

A few weeks after I got my licence, I met one of the councillors who always voted against me when I applied for a licence. I enjoyed winding him up, and to give him his due he took it well. We were having a chat in the street and I asked him if he had seen my latest application for a licence.

He told me he hadn't and said, 'I thought you had every licence possible for breaking the Sabbath.'

I answered, 'This will break the Sabbath all right – the application is for a crematorium.'

He made an about-turn and I could hear him muttering, 'You are a head-case all right!'

We still used to go down to London from time to time to visit family. On one occasion it was my wife's birthday and I had arranged for a room in a local restaurant in Sutton for the family to have a meal. Unfortunately she fell ill the day before her birthday. When I went to the restaurant to cancel the arrangements I had made, lo and behold, who was in there but Brian Siddle, a retired senior officer who also happened to be a close friend.

'Hello Jock,' he said, 'what are you doing down here? Are you going to join me for a glass of wine?'

I said, 'No, Brian, I am on a yellow line.'

Brian said, 'You have twenty minutes – you'll be OK.'

'In that case,' I said, 'I'll have two glasses!'

But when I went out there was a traffic warden with a £60 ticket. The same day I was on my mobile phone while driving. I clocked a panda car behind me, dropped my phone and carried on into Morrison's car park. The officer followed and stopped me. I couldn't fault his approach. He told me that he had seen me driving and using my phone. I answered him back in Gaelic. He asked another few questions and I kept replying in Gaelic. In the end he got on his radio and told the station he had what he believed to be a Romanian who could not speak a word of English and asked for an interpreter. I had to come clean as I fell over the panda car bonnet laughing.

The officer quite rightly didn't see the funny side, and issued me with a £60 fine with three points on my licence. Not a bad birthday present for my wife – £120 in fines on the same day!

By 1997 the pub was earning, and everything was sweet. Donalda and I decided to have a break and travel to Aberdeen to see the start of the Tall Ships Race.

Just prior to leaving for Aberdeen she had given blood. After a couple of days we had a call for her to go and see her GP as soon as we got back. When she was diagnosed with leukaemia, my world fell apart and I cried my eyes out. Donalda was and still is my rock. She was treated in Glasgow, and thankfully the leukaemia is in remission. I will always be grateful to the NHS and I couldn't fault the treatment she received.

After I retired I wanted to do something to repay the leukaemia unit (the Paul O'Gorman Unit) in the Beatson Centre in Glasgow which looked after Donalda. First of all I put a swearbox in the public bar, and anyone who swore in the pub had to put in a donation. Fred MacLennan and I were the biggest contributors. The swearbox raised £5,000 over the years.

I then decided as a finale I would do something outrageous – but what? At the time the 'Calendar Girls' were the talk of the town, so I thought, 'Why not the Calendar Boys?'

A few of us got together, and with the help of a friendly professional photographer called John MacLean, the 'Naked Hebridean Calendar' was born. This was so successful it made the national news. Mac TV followed us to London and made a documentary for the BBC. It raised a total of £32,000. A further £400 went towards the local lifeboat.

The Golden Age

Since I retired I have made more arrests and been in more scrapes than I ever was when I was serving in the force, albeit only in my dreams. There is not a night that I don't have some sort of dream in which I am arguing with a senior officer or fighting a bank robber. I had to move into another bed, as my wife woke up on several occasions in an arm-lock. The dreams are so vivid and faces of colleagues who have long since passed away appear as clearly as when I knew them.

When I was at Kennington, Detective Chief Inspector Bell said of me in his annual report, 'He leads with the force of a tornado.' These days have gone.

I am lucky to have a loving wife who has looked after me now for 47 years, to enjoy good health despite the way I abused my body, to have a wonderful family and to be surrounded by them and my eleven grandchildren. I enjoy my fishing and there is nothing I like more than reminiscing about the fantastic life I have had. I would choose exactly the same life over again.

I am afraid old age is creeping up, however. The ginger hair has gone white, the drams are getting smaller. The Golden Age has arrived.

Well, they say Senior Citizens are the nation's leading carriers of AIDS – hearing aids, band-aids, bath aids, walking aids, medical aids, sex aids, government aids and, most of all, monetary aids – for their children.

The Golden Years have come at last.
I cannot see, I cannot pee,
I cannot chew, I cannot screw,
My memory shrinks, my hearing stinks,
I cannot smell, I look like hell,
My body's drooping, I've got trouble pooping.
So the Golden Years have come at last?
Well, the Golden Years can kiss my ass!